# Debbie Fanning

# THE JOURNEY HOME

FINDING MY VOICE AND TAKING MY POWER
BACK AFTER A DEVASTATING ASSAULT

## THE JOURNEY HOME

First published in Great Britain in 2023

Copyright ©2023

Debbie Fanning has asserted her right under the Copyright Designs and Patents Act 1988 to be identified as the author of this work.

A CIP catalogue record for this book is available from the British Library.

This book is sold subject to the condition that it shall not by way of trade or otherwise be lent, resold, hired out or otherwise circulated without the publisher's prior consent in any form of binding or cover, other than that in which it is published and without a similar condition, including this condition being imposed on the subsequent purchaser.

Printed and bound in Great Britain

## To Lucy

～

Without you I would not have had the strength to
fight for my survival. You have given me a life I did not
know possible. As you grow into the amazing woman
I know you will be, I hope …

*That you will always know how special you are;*
*That you will always know your worth.*
*That you know that trying your best will always be enough.*
*That you will have the conviction to follow your dreams*

Love you forever xx

# Contents

Introduction

Acknowledgements:

Finding my tribe

Chapter

1. The me before 'what happened' ............................................. 1
2. What happened ........................................................................ 4
3. The days and weeks that followed ........................................ 8
4. Two pink lines ........................................................................ 12
5. Trying therapy ........................................................................ 16
6. IVF ............................................................................................ 23
7. Giving birth ............................................................................ 31
8. Lucy – my whole world ........................................................ 40
9. Triggered back into therapy ................................................ 44
10. Finding mindfulness ............................................................ 51
11. Madeleine Black .................................................................... 56
12. The full story of that night .................................................. 59
13. Remembering: the aftermath .............................................. 72
14. Telling my parents, at last .................................................... 74
15. 2020 – not another decade .................................................. 79
16. The Pandemic ........................................................................ 85
17. Going in... .............................................................................. 95
18. Acknowledging the grief ...................................................... 98
19. Dear younger self ................................................................ 101
20. Coping strategies ................................................................ 107
21. Body image .......................................................................... 112
22. Rewriting the script ............................................................ 116
23. The see me, hear me blog .................................................. 121
24. Reclaiming my body ............................................................ 130
25. The turning point – finding myself .................................. 136
26. Life begins at 40 .................................................................. 144
27. How I would help someone else ...................................... 147
28. I'll have the final say! My letter to the men who raped me ... 153
29. Moving on – the next chapter .......................................... 159

# Introduction

*'If there's a book that you want to read, but it hasn't been written yet, then you must write it.'* – Toni Morrison

For a long time, I have struggled with where to begin with my story. How could I possibly put into words the most abhorrent thing that could ever have happened to me? I have been silent and voiceless for so long, but now that I have found my voice again, I want to be able to share with others the assurance that no matter the magnitude of trauma, you can still come out the other side. No journey will be the same, and for me, it has taken me nearly two decades to get to this place, but now that I have, I hope that one day, my story could be someone else's survival guide.

As I begin to tell my story, I am speaking from a place where I never thought I would be. I saw a quote on social media which helped me decide how to start the journey of telling my story:

*'I didn't think I'd be able to laugh again, but I did. I didn't think I'd ever be ok but somehow it just happened. Life went on and beautiful times returned as time sifted through my fingers like a soft summer's breeze, and I was so grateful.'* - SC Lourie

Getting to this place of peace has felt like nothing short of a miracle. It has not simply been feeling a 'soft summer's breeze'. It has taken me nearly two decades to even remember what this feels like, but for the first time in a long time, I have been able to feel things other than fear, sadness and anxiety. When you have suffered any kind of trauma, no matter how significant, it alters your brain, your emotions and for me, your world. What happened to me was the worst thing that has ever happened in my life, and the recovery from it has been even harder.

My story is one of trauma, denial, disassociation, shame, guilt, self-hatred, self-harm and so much more that will unfold throughout the chapters that follow. But it also details a story of strength, determination, fight and most importantly HOPE, which is something a lot of survivors lose.

In a journey of nearly 20 years, I have been on a rollercoaster trying to navigate my way through the minefield of trauma. For those that have been through this or are currently doing so, you will know that it feels like wading through treacle. You feel stuck, you feel lost, you feel hopeless, and you feel alone in a world that nobody understands.

I have been plagued by so many emotions over the years, all of which I struggled to manage. But before I could begin to manage them, I had to accept them, I had to be able to identify them, and for that to happen, I had to be honest with myself. That was the hardest part.

I am now in place where I can say have come out of the darkness and found some light again, something I never thought possible. I have moved towards a place of acceptance and peace, realising that this healing journey may well be a lifelong process and I'm ok with that now. Connection has been my biggest saviour in this journey of survival to healing and I would not have got to this place without the connections I have made – with other people, and with myself. I want to be able to share my experience to let others know that there is hope, there is always hope, even when you may not see it or feel it. You can get to a place where life is good again, no matter how shattered your world has been.

# Acknowledgements: Finding my tribe

*'The most memorable people in your life will be the people who loved you when you weren't loving yourself.'* – Brigitte Nicole

There are certain people I will talk about through my story who have helped me immeasurably, and I could not be more grateful for their support. I have had a few friends who have come in at different points (when I felt I could trust them enough to let them in). I know it has been extremely difficult for them to watch me from the sidelines, often feeling helpless. True friends will ride that storm with you and see you come out the other side.

There are also people I have met along the way who have been so influential on my life that I truly believe I would not be here without them.

Firstly there is Trudy, my best friend, who was there with me from day 1 (or day 8, which was when I actually told her). At that time, Trudy was a colleague who I had grown particularly close with. She was the first person I told about what happened and has offered me comfort, love and support since the day I told her. We have become more than friends – I now class her as family. Trudy has seen me at my worst and still didn't leave. She was there for me at a drop of a hat for every meltdown, appointment and for the many times of despair. She has also been there for me in my biggest achievement to date – the birth of my beautiful daughter – and she and Lucy now share a bond that is special beyond words.

Trudy and I continue to be colleagues and friends and have come through this whole journey together. At times I have pushed her away and she has still came back for more. At times, I have retreated into myself in order to survive, but she was always there when I came back out. And now we are able to share good times with our gorgeous girls, making amazing memories as I come out of the other side.

Irene Campbell was the third counsellor I worked with. Irene established the CARA project (Challenging and Responding to Abuse) to support victims of domestic abuse, rape, sexual assault and sexual abuse. This service was a very small and much undervalued service that was run by three counsellors at the time. I instantly had a connection with Irene, unlike the previous two counsellors I had worked with. She was so warm, gentle, caring and compassionate. I could tell the counsellors I worked with who had had lived experience, as their whole manner of counselling was very different. She had a burning rage inside that wanted to see me get through what had happened and instil that fighting spirit back into me to move on to the next chapter of my life.

Irene and I worked together for two and a half years. I now know that I hadn't got anywhere near addressing or unpicking the trauma that was buried so deep within when we first worked together, but she got me to a place where I felt strong enough to make my own decisions, including the most important one of my life – choosing to have my little girl on my own. I owe Irene everything for helping me to achieve a dream that I thought had been stolen from me – the dream of becoming a mother. Unfortunately, my time with Irene came to an abrupt ending as sadly, she was diagnosed with cancer and died a few months later. The loss of Irene is something that will hurt forever, but when I think about her, I just look at my little girl and feel so immeasurably grateful that she was part of my journey.

Karen Laing was the fourth counsellor I worked with. I had

known of her from working with Irene at the CARA project and felt that she was someone I could possibly connect with on the same level. I developed an even closer relationship with Karen, if that was possible. We went through so much together, but I felt we were still very much right in the middle of things when our working relationship came to an end. Karen had to take some time off for personal reasons and I was not able to continue a working relationship with her when she returned, which I found extremely difficult. Karen had managed to get me to a deeper place of working through my trauma than I had ever been before.

I was lucky enough to find another amazing lady whilst I was still working with Karen. I met Lee McLaughlin when my friend Karen asked me if I wanted to try a mindfulness course. Lee was the facilitator of the course, which opened me up to a whole new world of healing strategies. I was fortunate that Lee also offered 1:1 coaching, and when my working relationship with Karen ended, she was able to offer me support. Like Irene and Karen, I don't think Lee knew what she was getting herself into when she agreed to help me.

Neither of us knew the depths we would get to in finally uncovering what had happened to me. I honestly do not know where I would be today without Lee's support. Like Karen and Irene, Lee has a special gift of kindness, compassion, knowledge and making you feel like the most important person in the room. The work I have done with her has taken me to places I never thought I would get to, and she is the reason I am able to write this book today.

Finally there is my one of my oldest friends, Karen McBride. We met in Primary 1 and have been friends ever since. We went to high school together, college together, got jobs in the same council and went to uni together, and she will always hold a special place in my heart. It was Karen's birthday that I was out celebrating the night my attack happened. For a long time, she has carried a lot of guilt about letting me leave on my own that night. She knows that the only people who were to blame for that night were the two men who chose to rape me – nobody else.

These five ladies will never know how much they mean to me and how much they have helped me to rebuild my life since it was left in tatters, and I would like to dedicate this book to them.

And finally to my friends, who have never given up, even when I may have disappeared for a while. You have always been there, no matter what point of my journey you came in on, loving me for who I was without question or judgement. I thank you for your love, your support, your friendship and your understanding. You know who you are.

CHAPTER 1

# The me before 'what happened'

*'You can't go back and change the beginning, but you can start where you are and change the ending' – C.S. Lewis*

Growing up, I had a fairly privileged upbringing. I was brought up by both parents and a younger brother. We lived in nice houses and I enjoyed school, had nice holidays and had lots of family and friends around me. My dad was the typical breadwinner of the family and often worked long hours to allow my mum not to have to go to work and raise my brother and me. My mum did not return to work until I was 19 years old, so she was there for us the whole way through school. I never had to worry about going to breakfast club or afterschool and would always get chauffeured to and from school. I did have it very easy. But I often joke that my parents got off lightly with me too! I did well at school, didn't drink before I was 18, had a good friend group and never really caused them any hassles – although they may say different!

I had always been a fairly shy and quite girl. I'd never had a real boyfriend and tended to keep myself within my own wee circle, both at school and at home. From a very young age, I had a clear plan in my head about what my future would look like. I would get married in my early 20s and have two children, just like what my family looked like. Like most young girls, I had my wedding planned in my head – what my dress would look like, how many bridesmaids I would have, where it would be. I also had names for the two children I was going to have, a boy and a girl.

I had always loved being around children, which led me into the career that I am in today. I chose to study Early Learning and Childcare at college, and that was where my career path started. As with school, I was very dedicated to my studies and made sure I put everything I had into doing a good job. I was teased for being super organised and quite anal about getting things done in a certain way and on time. I was lucky enough to get a job in the nursery that I had been a student in and was loving the direction my life was taking.

My twenty-first year was the happiest time I had ever had. I turned 21 in October 2002 and celebrated with a big party. It was really out of my comfort zone to have a party and be the centre of attention, but I ended up loving every minute of it and having the best time. The buzz I felt from my party carried on to the following week when I went for my first trip to New York. I was on cloud 9 and living my best life. I had been desperate to go to New York for so long and finally had the chance to experience it with my mum.

New York did not disappoint and I had the most amazing six days, falling in love with New York even more. I was like in a kid in a candy shop exploring all the different places. Admittedly, I was a bit of a designer addict at the time when it came to clothes, so walking down Fifth Avenue was like a dream come true, and I felt like a movie star. We visited all of the tourist sites that we had time to cram into our six days. Times Square was just buzzing with life, Central Park was so peaceful and beautiful, the Empire State building was phenomenal, and I could not get enough of the feeling I got from being in this amazing city. The smell of nuts from the little carts on the corner of the streets, the steam coming up from the manholes in the middle of the street, the sound of the taxis honking their horns at all hours of the day... I just loved every minute of it and felt so lucky to have got the opportunity to visit. My mum and I literally shopped till we dropped and came back from our trip totally exhausted. We both then developed a common love of New York, and this was to be the first of many of our trips together.

Heading into Christmas of that year, my life could not have been going any better. I had met someone who I was in the early days of seeing and felt all my plans were coming to fruition. I felt happy, I felt content, I had nothing to worry about and I was excited about my future.

This was the last time I remember feeling anything like that. My world was about to be turned upside down and inside out. The life I was living was about to end, and take a whole new direction.

CHAPTER 2

# 'What happened'

*'Trauma, quite simply, can be defined as life-threatening powerlessness.' – Carolyn Spring*

For a long time, I referred to my traumatic event as 'what happened'. I could not use the word 'rape' and didn't know why until very recently. I simply would say, 'after what happened to me'. Yet 'what happened to me' was in fact gang rape and attempted murder. I have only become aware of the magnitude of that night in the last few years, as until then I had disassociated from the attack. My mind and body were frozen in time, which was what helped me to survive the attack, but it was also what nearly killed me again when I finally allowed myself to work through the trauma.

My memories of that night were very blurred and did not always make sense to me, so I am going to start off with how I remembered the night at the time.

On Saturday the 25$^{th}$ of January (Burns Night) 2003, I was out for the night celebrating the 21$^{st}$ birthday of one of my best friends, Karen. We started the night at her house, having a few drinks, then we had a limo arranged to take us into town to celebrate. The night started off full of laughs and fun, with us thinking we were movie stars riding into town in a limo.

After having dinner and going to a nightclub, I began to feel unwell, so I left to go and get a taxi. I remember crossing the road and starting to walk down Queen Street. Debenhams was right in front of me, so I knew the taxi rank was right underneath it. Then, out of nowhere, I felt an overwhelming sense that there was someone behind me. Before I had a chance to look round, I felt a hand come over my mouth and nose and felt myself being lifted off the ground. Everything was so dark and I very quickly became overwhelmed with panic and fear. I had no idea what was happening or what was about to happen.

I ended up at the bottom of the lane, my face pushed against a wall. I could not see anything, but was hyper-aware of sounds that were echoing through my brain. On this dark, cold night in the centre of Glasgow where you should be hearing people coming and going about their night, I heard one sound only that immediately transported me to a level of fear like I had never known. It was the sound of a zip. It's a sound you are probably never aware of hearing as you get dressed and undressed every day, but it pierced my ears as I suddenly realised what was going to happen.

I next remembered being pushed onto the ground, the cold, freezing ground, and there the rape took place.

Whilst I was lying on the ground, another man appeared.

I thought he had maybe seen me being dragged down the lane and was there to rescue me. Sadly, this was not the case. He was there to join in. I thought I was going to die, that I would never see my family and friends again. I remember pain that you could never describe, and that's what was really hard for me. I knew in my head what the pain was like, but I somehow felt disconnected from it and couldn't find any words to describe it. I remember panic taking over my body and feeling like I was having an outer body experience.

After it was over, I was told to lie there and not move or they would come back and kill me. When you are in so much shock and consumed with that level of fear, you believe anything, and for many years, I still believed this to be true.

I lay for what felt like an eternity before trying to move. As I got myself up and headed towards the end of the lane, my nightmare continued. The second man who had appeared during the attack emerged from behind three large industrial bins. I was dragged back to the end of the lane and the attack resumed.

This part of the attack has been the bit that haunted me the most. They said they would do something if I didn't listen – and they did. If I had listened, they wouldn't have come back. I made it worse for myself, it was my fault. All these thoughts spiralled out of control in my head and added to the tsunami of guilt and shame that I lived with for years.

When I finally got up to leave the second time, I headed out towards Queen Street. I could see the Debenhams sign again and knew that I was close to the taxi rank. I eventually got into a taxi and headed home. From this point, I had decided that I would never tell anyone about it. The rape had never happened. It had all been a bad dream.

My memories back then were so vague that this was the only description I had for 'what happened' that night. Very little detail, very little emotion and very few words to describe the reality.

A part of me died that night.

CHAPTER 3

# The days and weeks that followed

*'All it takes is a beautiful fake smile to hide an injured soul and they will never notice how broken you are.' – Robin Williams*

When the taxi dropped me off, I opened the front door to find nobody was home. My mum was working a night shift and my dad and brother were both out. I immediately headed for the shower and stayed in there for what seemed like an eternity. No amount of soap and hot water could make me feel clean. My body didn't feel my own any more. I felt dirty, disgusting, and my skin was crawling. The water pouring down my legs turned red as it mixed with blood. I watched it in slow motion swirl down the drain, along with my dignity, my self-worth and my soul.

What do you do when something like this happens? The only way I knew how to survive was to pretend it hadn't happened. Knowing now the injuries I had received, I have no idea how I was able to carry on as 'normal'. My brain had literally shut off from what had happened. I was in pain, I was still bleeding, but my body and brain didn't seem to register these two things together and thankfully, this allowed me to carry on.

It was never an option for me to contact the police. I had decided the minute I made it out of that lane that I could never tell anyone, let alone the police. The threats that had been made had already silenced me I couldn't contemplate the thought of any sort of physical examination. I have since been asked lots of times why I didn't contact the police, and I feel that this is such a personal choice. I stand by my decision not to report it one hundred percent. What victims have to go through in the reporting process and into the judicial process is a trauma in itself, and for me it was one that I could not face then and still don't think I could face today. It is very sad that victims of rape or sexual assault feel this way. So much needs to change in our legal processes to make women sufficiently validated, listened to, comfortable and supported to do this.

I went back to work on the Monday morning. Working in a nursery with over 50 three to five-year-olds, there was no other option but to be happy, cheery and upbeat. I have one vivid memory of pain from that first day back at work and it was when I bent down to pick a child up. A piercing pain shot right through me as if something had torn. I remember a few of my colleagues looking at me at the time, but I shrugged it off and continued with my work. A few people had asked if I was ok, saying I didn't seem myself. I simply told them I was fine and carried on.

Carrying on was something I became very good at. I had too. Those few weeks after the attack are a total blur. I was in shock, I was in denial. I had no idea who this person was that was walking about with a body that didn't feel like her own any more, yet everything still had to be 'normal.'

Losing myself has been the greatest tragedy of my trauma. I lost the life I had and the life I was going to have, and felt stuck in a parallel universe where the world continued moving and I was stuck, stuck in a hell that I couldn't explain. To the outside world I was carrying on, but I was falling apart on the inside. Nothing seemed to connect for me any more. My emotions didn't match what my body was feeling. I would smile, but feel nothing. I could not cry, yet I felt as if my insides were sobbing. My brain felt like it was going to explode, yet it felt empty and in a blur. The attack was not only physical; it was an attack on my psyche, and that has been the hardest part of all to deal with.

Two weeks later my friend Trudy (who I drove to work every day), asked me if something had happened. She said that she and a few other people had noticed bruising on my back when I bent over. I can't remember much of what I told her at that time, but I did tell her that yes, something had happened. I remember feeling terrified telling her, as the two men had said that if I told anyone, they would come and find me and do it again. I made Trudy promise not to tell anyone, and she agreed.

A few weeks after that, I told some more of the girls I worked with. They were beyond supportive, but starting to worry about my health. Trudy persuaded me to tell my boss at the time, which is one of the worst decisions I made. My boss was already quite a controlling, authoritative figure, with clear deep emotional issues of her own. I remember sitting at her desk telling her that something had happened. Her reaction still haunts me now, but looking through a trauma-informed lens, I can see that this was more to do with her issues than it was with mine. She put her head in her hands, letting out a scream, then walked out of the office, slamming the door on me. The shame and guilt amplified in my mind. Why had I told her? I could not trust her not to share it with anyone. I felt terrified again that my story might come out. For days after, she would ignore me, walk out of the staffroom as I walked in, slam doors whenever I was around. It was horrible and I felt more than ever that this was my fault and I was the one that had done something wrong.

Work, which had been my safe place, then became a very difficult place to be. This was the one place that I could keep busy and put a show on to prove everything was 'normal'. I didn't want to be at home because if I had time to stop, I might start thinking, and the thought of that was too unbearable. Thankfully, that manager left and moved onto another nursery, but the reaction of this lady altered my thinking even more about telling anyone what had happened.

When we were en route to work most days Trudy would try and get me to open up about what happened, but I just didn't have the words. I didn't even have any emotions. I felt like I should be crying and at times felt desperate to cry for some sort of relief, but nothing would come out. I didn't know then that when I did start crying, I was never going to stop.

CHAPTER 4

# Two pink lines

*'It's hard to sleep when your heart is at war with your mind.' – R H Sim*

As the weeks went by, I continued to live in the hell inside my head and body, yet I still couldn't articulate what any of this was. I was in a constant state of fear and anxiety, on a rollercoaster that had no stop button. I could not sleep, I could not eat, but I continued on as if nothing had happened in the outside world.

When I thought things couldn't get any worse, they did. I don't know what made me do it as I was still in a state of denial, but on some level, I knew something else wasn't right. I took a pregnancy test and it came back positive. Two pink lines! I wanted to burst into floods of tears, but I still couldn't cry. How could this be happening? Even the fake world that I had built around my trauma was about to come crumbling down.

I can't remember the exact date I took the pregnancy test; I'm not even sure what made me take it or what made my mind even go there. I vaguely remember something about the blood loss I had suffered and because it hadn't really stopped, I started to wonder if this had merged into a period. The test confirmed that it had not. I can't properly describe how I felt when I saw those two little lines. I had dreamed about being a mum for as long as I could remember, but not like this.

My feelings were very mixed up at this time and I feel I was in a constant state of (hidden) fear, however I feel that this was the point when that it escalated higher. I remember thoughts of, 'how can I hide this? People will know my secret', 'if I tell people, 'they' will come back' and 'how can I look after a baby, I can't look after myself?' And even, 'if I said I had had a one-night stand, then this baby might make all the other pain go away.'

Nothing at all made sense. I mentally could not process any more information, I knew that I could not go through with a termination, for many reasons; I could not cope with any physical procedure, because then people would know what had happened. I never saw abortion as an option for me. I totally agree with pro-choice and understand why people make this decision, but for me, it was more about *not* acknowledging what happened.

The disgust and loathing I felt about my body was only compounded by the thought of a little baby being in my tummy. Not anything about the baby itself, more that I would never want a baby to grow inside me as I was so disgusting and damaged that a beautiful baby deserved better than that. I vaguely remember having some thoughts about a wee tiny baby being in my arms, and I always thought of it as a 'she'. Maybe if it could work and I could focus on this rather than the other stuff, it could help me get over 'it', but this was a fantasy that could never be reality.

Thinking back, I had worked out that I would have been 5-6 weeks pregnant when I took the test. The mental torment I put myself through about what to do for the best was what pushed me to breaking point. And that point meant I could no longer face the physical and mental pain that had become my life. If I was no longer here, I would not have to make any choices about what happened to this baby and we would both be in a better place. I remember writing a note to my mum and dad and Trudy, apologising for what I had done (or meant to have done). I then drove to a very remote place and took too many tablets.

Later the following morning I remember walking up in the car, feeling horrendous, and started vomiting everywhere. I remember feeling devastated that it had not worked and I was still here, facing the same pain that I so longed to make disappear. I don't know how I managed to drive home, but I did, and I was in bed for days after that. I had terrible pains in my stomach, but I thought this was due to the amount of tablets I had taken. This may well be the case, but I also now know that this was probably part of what was to be a miscarriage. I have no memory of what date it happened, but I started bleeding really heavily and very differently from the bleeding after the trauma I had suffered. I knew then that not only had I failed to take the pain away for myself, but I had taken a life away from an innocent little baby. I cannot describe how heartbroken I felt. If possible, I hated myself for that even more.

I began fantasising about what it would have been like to

have a baby girl. I wouldn't have cared about how she came into this world, I would have loved her, because she was mine and she would have turned my life away from the trauma and pain I had endured. The inward self-hatred, self-loathing, guilt, shame and disgust I felt could not be challenged or resolved, as I never told anyone. Not only was I hiding a massive secret, I had to stop myself grieving for a loss that I felt I didn't have a right to grieve for.

CHAPTER 5

# Trying therapy

*'PTSD isn't about what's wrong with you, it's about what happened to you.'*

Trying to recover from the miscarriage physically and mentally on my own was so hard. I had to learn to do what I had done with my trauma that night – shut it away. I kept busy, I didn't allow myself to think or feel and I soon disassociated from this too.

As the year progressed, I was rapidly sinking into a dark place, whilst still looking to everyone else as if nothing had happened. Some nights I would choose to sleep in my car, as I couldn't bear being in my bedroom, where the memories seemed to come alive.

By this stage, I had told a GP what had happened. I remember her speaking to me and referring to 'the alleged assault.' This only confirmed the thinking in my head that no one would believe me. Surely my word and the state that I was in were enough for her to believe me? My attempts to trust professionals had not got off to a great start, and the more professionals I spoke to, the more this continued.

I eventually agreed to a referral for counselling. It took me so long to agree to this that I naively thought I would be seen the next week. Unfortunately, I was put on a 16-week waiting list. Considering the amount of energy it had taken to get myself to a place where I would even consider talking to someone, being told I would need to wait another four months just devastated me. I put my walls back up and said I wasn't doing it.

By the time the appointment came through, Trudy had persuaded me to just try it and go, I had nothing to lose. I remember feeling absolutely paralysed by fear as I was called into the room. My body seemed to carry me, even though my mind was screaming at me not to go. Needless to say, the appointment did not go well. I said to my GP when she made the appointment that I would go as long as I didn't need to tell them what happened. She reassured me that they would get to know me first and move forward at my pace. The first thing the counsellor said to me was, 'why don't you tell me you are here today?' That was enough for my body and mind to connect, and I ran out the room. It was the one thing I had said I didn't want to do, and this just confirmed in my mind that I wasn't meant to talk about this.

That experience put me off attempting therapy again for a number of years. By then I had developed my own ways of coping silently. I stopped eating, or would eat and be sick. I did not see this as an eating disorder, I just blamed it on anxiety and having no appetite, but this was one of the many things I was in denial about. I had also started to use cutting as a way of coping when things got too intense for my brain to handle. Not many people understand this aspect of self-harming, but for me, it was a way of getting out of my head and bringing me back to reality – letting me feel real pain rather than the pain I was feeling in my head.

About three or four years later, the nightmares I was experiencing were so horrific that I would choose not to sleep in order to avoid them. I was managing four or five nights with no sleep before my body gave in and I had to allow the nightmares to happen in order to sleep. I finally spoke this through with my GP, who persuaded me to accept a referral to the Sandyford Sexual Assault Counselling Service. I tried to go into this counselling with more of an open mind. I was feeling desperate for someone to help me, as I felt I couldn't go on much longer.

Trudy was allowed to come into the sessions with me, which really helped. The lady who saw me was nice enough, but I still had so many barriers up that she would never have got through. I attended for months before she suggested that we try something called EMDR (eye movement desensitization and reprocessing therapy). This type of therapy would focus on altering the memories I had stored in the brain but had not processed.

I agreed, and had about 10 sessions of what I can only describe as the most intense thing I had ever experienced. I remember my body feeling as if it was not my own again. I was sitting in a room and feeling like I was in a war zone, fighting for my life. I now know that this was my body's way of trying to process the feelings and memories I had of that night – which did include fighting for my life. Many of these sessions resulted in me fainting and being picked up off the floor by Trudy and the therapist.

I wouldn't say that I ever truly connected with this therapist. I went because I was desperate, but I started getting used to her. It was helping with my nightmares, so I tolerated going, even though I felt terrible before and after each session. I never ever spoke to her about what happened, which was why I continued going. She was literally helping me cope with getting through each day.

Then, just as I had accepted that she was actually an ok person and was helping me, she told me that she was leaving her post and that another therapist would be taking over from her. Immediately all my defences went back up. How had I allowed myself to feel semi-comfortable with someone for them then to be taken away? My distrust for service providers came back, along with my overwhelming feelings of 'why did you give away your secret?' Although I hadn't told anyone what had actually happened, I had let someone else into my mind and this didn't feel like a safe thing to do any more.

I tried working with the new therapist, but I had switched off again and that window of maybe letting someone in had been shut. I tried a few sessions, then didn't go back.

In October 2010 I had reached a place where I could see for myself that I needed help, without someone having to talk me into it. My friend had set me up on a blind date (the first time I'd ever contemplated being around a man since it happened). We went out on a few dates and saw each other for a few months. I just couldn't connect or let him near me. It quickly fizzled out, as he more or less said that I wasn't going quickly enough for him. This set me into a new panic about never getting the chance to be a mum. If I couldn't even kiss a man, how on earth was I going to be able to have a baby? I wasn't even that interested in being in a relationship – I just wanted to be a mum.

This time, I decided for myself that I needed help and took some ownership in deciding where would be the best place to go. The last two services had been chosen for me, so this time I had to find somewhere that felt right. A friend of mine had suggested a lady called Irene who she knew from a service called the CARA project, which specialised in challenging and responding to abuse. I did some researching about the service. At first I didn't think it was suitable for what I had gone through as it detailed helping women experiencing domestic violence and victims of abuse. I didn't class myself in those categories.

I realised that it had been easier for my GP to make the referrals previously as it meant that I hadn't had to acknowledge anything. I got her telephone number from my friend, who could not speak highly enough of her. I wished I could have emailed her rather than speaking to her on the phone as that would mean I would have to say out loud what happened. I found the courage from somewhere and called her, saying that I needed some support after 'an attack'.

I had an instant connection with Irene. She was so warm and

caring she seemed to get right away that I didn't want to talk about anything (yet!) Irene spent time getting to know me. She never rushed me; she totally followed my lead and was able to read me better than anyone had up until that point.

I worked with Irene for about a year and a half before I was able to start putting into words what had happened. Even then, I still very much had boundaries about how far I would go. I remember one of the first things we worked on was my feelings of guilt and shame. Irene was able to tease things out of me without me even feeling like I was opening up about anything. We worked for months and months on this until one day I was finally able to see for myself that this was not my fault. This had been the first time in nearly 10 years that I had ever allowed that thought to enter my head. I began to feel a wee bit of space inside, like something had gone.

I was never able to tell Irene the fully story of what happened. At that time, I still could not find words for a lot of it and I actually had not processed a lot of the memories. Irene supported me through to my 30th birthday, which was a real trigger for me. I had associated big birthdays with terrible things happening. I remembered that feeling of having pure happiness, only for it to be taken away, and I was convinced that when I turned 30, this was going to happen again. Of course this didn't happen and I was able to celebrate my birthday and enter a new decade. It was at this point I decided that I had to start taking control of my life, and this was going to begin with me deciding to be a mum.

I was sitting in my hairdresser's salon, LJF, and we were

talking about men and children and life. She asked me if I had ever thought of having children and I said it was my dream to become a mum, but I just hadn't met the right person and didn't think I ever would. She told me about her cousin, who had decided to have a baby on her own by using a sperm donor. I always say to Lorna (who is now one of my closest friends) that this was the conversation that changed my life.

I spoke to Irene about this being a possibility for me and she helped me work through all the options and the implications and practicalities. For the first time, I felt in a place where I was ready to take control and finally do something for me. This time was very bitter sweet for me, as Irene suddenly fell ill and was not able to see me through the next part of this journey. Irene sadly died in September 2013 after a short battle with cancer. Losing her was like losing a family member. She had been the first person I had finally opened up to and really had a strong bond with. To this day, Irene holds such a huge part of my heart, and I do believe that Lucy would not be here today if it had not been for her support.

CHAPTER 6

# IVF

*'A dream is a wish your heart makes' – Cinderella*

Being a mum had been a dream of mine for as long as I can remember. Even as a child I remember thinking that I would be a mum of two children when I grew up – a boy and a girl. As I got older, I just assumed that becoming a mum would be a natural progression in my life. I loved children so much and would always be babysitting or doing things with other people's kids, so much so that I shaped my career around my love of children.

One of the many things that was stolen from me that night was my dream of becoming a mother. How could I ever be a mum now? I had lost the one and only chance I could ever have and I knew that I would never be able to let a man anywhere near me again, so that light had blown out, along with my dream.

Nearly 10 years later, after a failed attempt at a relationship and two years of counselling, I had a conversation with my hairdresser, who has since become a close friend. I always say to her that this was the conversation that changed my life. Sitting in the chair in the salon, we were chatting normally and started talking about kids. I told her that I had been desperate to be a mum, but had accepted that it just wasn't meant to be as I didn't want to be in a relationship with anyone. She then told me that her cousin had just given birth to a baby girl with the help of a sperm donor. We spoke about how amazingly brave her cousin was to forget the rules and social norms of society and just follow her dreams. This conversation really planted a seed in my mind. Maybe my dreams hadn't disintegrated after all.

After nearly two years of playing every scenario through in my mind and talking it through with my counsellor, Trudy and some close friends, I decided to make some enquiries. Throughout those two years I must have felt in my head that this could be a serious option as I had started to save; I knew that if I did decide to go through with this, it would not be cheap. On the 27th of January (which I've just realised was Karen's birthday - the Karen who I was out with that night!) I had my first consultation.

I remember feeling engulfed with nerves. What if it was a man, what if they refused me, what if I needed tests done there and then? Every possible worry or fear that I could have had about this appointment I had. But something inside got me to that appointment. I got through it and I had a tiny glimmer of hope that my dreams could actually become a reality.

The doctor explained the processes, the costs and the timescales and said we could start after my next period. Then the fear kicked in. I wasn't ready for it to be that quick! I told him

I needed to time to plan and really think about it. He just told me to contact his secretary if and when I was ready to go ahead with it.

I left the appointment both excited and terrified. I couldn't believe that having the opportunity to be a mum was within my reach again. But the reality of how I would tell my mum and dad, explain to other people how it happened and get through the procedures was all whizzing around my brain. I decided not to tell anyone other than Trudy that I was going ahead with it. I didn't really want anyone's opinions on why I should or shouldn't do it. This was the first time in a very long time that it felt right, and I was so sure of my decision that I didn't want anyone to get in the way of it.

I have often said that the whole IVF process was a bit of blur to me, but as I sat down to write about it, I actually remembered more of the details than I thought I would. What I don't remember though is much of the emotion that I felt alongside it. I do believe that I didn't have the ability to connect with anything back then, as I was so disconnected from myself and not allowing myself to feel any emotion. I can now see that this was an automatic response from my trauma – just keep going, pretend everything is OK and you will get to the end. And for me, that end goal of having a baby was way bigger than any fear I could ever feel.

I do remember feeling really anxious before every appointment, to the point where I would be vomiting the night before with worry about what they were going to do, what examination I would have to endure and how I would control my reactions. I was worried that if these doctors could see how much I was affected by my trauma, they wouldn't let me go ahead with the IVF process in case I wasn't a fit mother.

My first internal scan was probably the worst. I knew it was coming and what I was in the waiting room for. My head was screaming *just leave, just go back in the lift before they call your name and get back to the car*. But somehow, my body took me into the room and got me undressed and lying on the bed before I could even process what I had done. This seemed to happen quite a lot; my body would go on automatic pilot to get me through situations that I deemed might be a threat.

I remember looking at the long probe and thinking, *how on earth is that going to fit inside me?* I had not processed all of the memories I had at this point, but I did know where that memory would take me if I connected to fact that this internal probe was going inside me.

None of the nurses knew anything about my trauma, but I think they could see how terrified I was. I remember an auxiliary nurse telling me to put my legs in the stirrups and get used to getting comfortable with feeling uncomfortable! She held my hand and talked me through what was happening. I remember the sharp pain as the nurse inserted the probe as I had tensed my body up so tightly, and the feeling of pressure as she moved it about to see each ovary. I don't really remember much detail about what they were looking for or what they were doing; I just remember looking at the ceiling praying for it to be over, something that felt hauntingly familiar.

The parts I remember most about the IVF are the procedures. I know I had other appointments that were just taking bloods, talking about medication, signing forms etc., but I have no clue what went on in them. Looking back on it now, I could have been signing and agreeing to anything.

There are so many questions that I wish I had asked at the time, but I was just so desperate to get to the end of the process without my trauma seeping out and again ruining my chances of being a mum. I was terrified the doctors would have a view of my mental health that I could not cope with a child, and I was more determined than ever to make sure I looked like I had my shit together.

I wish I had asked more about the implications for Lucy – what rights would she have, what rights would the sperm donor have, would there be a way that either could contact each other, what would happen with my frozen eggs, but all of these things I didn't even consider, I just needed to keep going and get to the other side.

I remember the point when the injections started. I had such a fear of needles that I had to have Trudy inject me daily. The injections made the size of my stomach double, and I was terrified that someone would notice my swelling belly. I felt as if my ovaries were about to explode. Latterly, as the injections had started, the internal scans became more frequent as they checked the size of the eggs. At one point, I remember having three internal scans in 1 week. I still cannot comprehend how I was able to do this and still go on with my day to day life (and keep this from everybody!) I remember my eggs having to be at what they called size 17 before they could do the egg retrieval. It seemed to take ages for them to get to this number, which is why I had to have more internal scans to check on it, but the eggs finally got to 17 and my egg retrieval was booked.

All of my appointments had been in the Princess Royal, but the surgery part of it was in the Nuffield Hospital. I arrived the morning of my appointment with Trudy, who was supporting me through it. I was sick with fear at this point. I was so scared to be sedated and not be in control of what was going on, and I knew Trudy would not be allowed into theatre with me. We went inside the hospital and it was like a hotel. We were taken to a private room which had its own private bathroom, a bed, comfy chair, plasma TV on the wall (not your typical NHS hospital). I have no recollection of any conversations with doctors or nurses at this point – everything is a blur. I remember them wheeling me on the bed to the theatre and being surprised that the theatre room was just across the hall from my private room. It seemed bizarre, but that's where my memory of that part of the procedure ends.

Five days later I was back in the Nuffield for the insemination. The physical part of this procedure I remember more than any other part of the treatment. I was wheeled back across to the same theatre room, but this time I was awake. A male doctor was in the room with Trudy and me, and I had the hospital gown on with no pants. The doctor asked me to lie on the bed and put my legs into the stirrups. I remember lying completely flat this time. With all the other scans I had been slightly raised on the bed, but not this time. I felt really uncomfortable and was dying for it to be over. I only had the hospital gown on, no sheet over me, and he pushed the gown up towards my stomach. I remember feeling horrified. He had completely exposed me without even trying to protect my dignity. I pushed it back down a bit to cover myself, but he pushed it back again. He then inserted the speculum, opening it wider to the point where I thought I was going to pass out.

Tears were trickling silently down my face and thought I was going to be sick, but he didn't listen. He never spoke to me or reassured me or anything. He uttered a few words that he was nearly done and then he loosened it and took it out. This was one part that I did feel really emotional about. I remember being back in the room crying and feeling so shaky. I had no verbal memories of my trauma and emotions that I was able to articulate back then. This was another memory that was hauntingly familiar, but I did not have the insight at the time to understand why.

I remember driving home after the procedure (even though you weren't meant to drive) and just acting as if nothing had happened. I spent the afternoon in bed at Trudy's, purely because I was too scared something would fall out.

The next 12 days were torture. The 12$^{th}$ day seemed as if it was never going to come. I tried really hard not to let myself imagine that my dreams could become a reality. I was in so much pain internally and in my pelvis. I was pumped so full of hormones that I felt like a total basket case. I had been given pessaries as part of the treatment to take up until the 12$^{th}$ day. They made me feel so disgusting and swollen that by day 9, I had

had enough. I could not use them any more. I remember thinking that I didn't care any more if the treatment had worked, I was just so desperate to feel better.

Day 12 came and I went round to Trudy's before work. I was convinced it hadn't worked, so I had prepared myself for a negative test and just to go back to work as normal. I had decided that I could never go through with another round of IVF, so that was my chance over. I sat at Trudy's kitchen table waiting for the result to come back. It seemed like an eternity, but after a few minutes, I had a look and there they were, those two pink lines that changed my life and made me realise that my dreams might now become a reality.

My reaction was of shock and disbelief. I could not believe it had worked. I felt like I should have cried or jumped for joy or something, but I just sat there thinking, *omg, this has worked!*

I can see now that this is where disassociation helped me to cope and keep going with my life. I'm not sure I would be able to go through that procedure again knowing what I know now, so I see it as a blessing that I had not processed these memories at the time or I might never have been able to pursue my dreams.

CHAPTER 7

# Giving birth

*'She was powerful not because she wasn't scared, but because she went on so strongly, despite the fear.'* – Atticus

It was Easter Monday and as awful as it is to say, this was the day I had dreaded since finding out I was pregnant. Terrified did not come close to how scared I was about going into hospital. I had never stayed in hospital on my own before and had never been admitted to hospital as an adult.

I was due to be at the Southern General Hospital for 2pm. Everything was organised, I had nothing left to pack, nothing left to sort out for coming home, nothing left to watch on TV – and even if I did, I couldn't sit still long enough. I had not slept the night before, but I didn't feel tired, I just felt the need to move. I had been out power-walking all week in a bid to get this baby moving to avoid being induced, but to no avail. I decided to go out in a last-ditch attempt to get her moving. I powered down the hill and along the road. All week I had thought my pelvis was going to split in two with the weight of her head on it, but still nothing.

Trudy came around about 1 pm. We had a cup of tea, then decided just to go. A garage conversion had literally been completed the night before, so I hadn't really had a chance to enjoy my own wee haven. I remember looking into the immaculate room and thinking, *I'll never get to enjoy this on my own again.* I looked in her little Moses basket that I had in the room and couldn't quite imagine a tiny person being inside it.

My dad had already left to go to the pub and hadn't said good luck or anything, so I was wasn't best pleased! He must have sensed my vibes, as he phoned me on the way to the hospital to wish me luck. My mum dropped Trudy and me off at the door and said she would come back and get Trudy later. I remember thinking, *please just take me back with you, I don't think I can do this.* During my whole pregnancy I had got away with only one internal examination. The midwife who did it was so lovely, and I had built up a really good relationship with her. She knew what had happened and was totally in tune with my cues for when to stop. She had passed information onto the hospital, but I wasn't holding out much hope of the same level of patience and understanding, as I knew how busy these places were.

When we got up to the ward, the midwife came in and put me on a monitor. She explained that she had spoken to Allison (my midwife) and was aware that I was probably terrified right now. I felt a bit of relief at this point. She said she would come back in half an hour to put the first pessary in. That little bit of relief vanished, and I began to feel sick and dizzy. Trudy told me to lie on the bed and try and close my eyes for half an hour. As you can imagine, that did not happen.

The nurse came back and put the first pessary in. As she was doing it, I remember crying. I don't know why, it wasn't overly painful, but I couldn't help it. After she had done that, she said we could go a walk, do what we wanted, but to be back by 6pm to have some dinner. I would get the next pessary about 10pm. I thought, OK that's fine, Trudy will still be there because she didn't need to leave until 1030.

We walked around the hospital for hours and went back at 6pm. We had something to eat and for the next few hours we just read magazines. I could see the clock getting near to 10pm, and I could feel my heart getting faster. Trudy tried to get me to put my pyjamas on before they came in but I protested and said, no no, I'm fine in my clothes. I felt that putting on pjs was a sign that I was staying, and I wasn't ready to think about that yet.

10pm came and went and then the bell rang for people to leave. I asked the midwife if someone was coming to put the other pessary in whilst Trudy was there, but she said they had been caught up and someone would be along soon. I remember walking Trudy to the lift. I was trying to act strong and not cry, but the minute the lift door closed, I felt an immense sense of fear that something terrible was going to happen again. I went back into my bed and lay crying into the pillow. A new midwife came in to put the other pessary in. She wasn't as gentle and didn't really say much when doing it. I kind of zoned out a bit and don't really remember much after that.

My first contraction started about 11.30pm, but it was just

mild cramping. By about 2pm they were stronger and coming on every six minutes. I had been texting Trudy to make sure she was on standby to get over to the hospital as soon as I needed her. She told me to ask for some paracetamol to try and take the edge off the pain. I was really reluctant to ask, as I thought if this was just the start of it, how was I going to cope when they got stronger? I finally gave in and the nurse brought me some cocodamol. It must have taken the edge off enough to make me doze off. I woke up half an hour later to hear a girl screaming down the corridor, then being rushed through the double doors beside my room. I could feel the colour drain out of me. I remember thinking, *holy fuck! Why do people do this?* I put my headphones in and listened to a 'labour playlist' that I had made.

By 4am the pain had become so intense that I was finding it difficult to manage. The nurse said she couldn't give me anything else, but I could try a bath. She came and got me when the bath was ready. It was in a big room at the end of the corridor. I remember her saying to me to keep the door open. I only lasted about 10 minutes in the bath and then started to feel faint. I remember lying on the cold floor with just the towel round me thinking I was going to pass out. I got myself back in my feet and dragged myself back to my bed.

I lay there for what seemed an eternity, listening to the bloody clock ticking on the wall. I remember thinking, *just get to 6am and they will check you and give you the other pessary.* All my fear about this had gone out of the window. I was just desperate to get to 2 cm so they could take me to the labour ward and break my water and Trudy could come back.

It was 9am before someone came round to check. By then, all contractions had stopped. I was gutted. I was convinced I was going to need the other pessary and have to wait another 6 hours. A young midwife with dark hair came and sat on the bed. She said she was going to check me and try and give me a sweep before putting the next pessary in. This was so incredibly painful – I felt like her whole hand was inside me. When she pulled her hand out, I could see her glove covered in blood. She said that she had released the mucus plug and I was 2 cm, so I could get ready to go to the labour ward.

Trudy came up about 10.20. I felt exhausted by then, so she told me to try and shut my eyes as she rubbed my arm. I must have dozed off again. By 11.30, I was ready to go to the labour ward.

We got to the labour suite and I remember thinking, this room is tiny! There was literally just enough room for the bed, some monitors, the baby crib and a chair. I don't remember anything about the midwife other than her being overly cheery. She told me she would be with me until 7pm, but she didn't think she would be the one delivering my baby. She said she was just going on her lunch, so she would let me get settled and when she came back she would break my waters.

Ten minutes later, another midwife came in and said there had been a change of plan and she was going to break my waters now. I got into position, grabbed Trudy's hand and braced myself for the pain. In actual fact, it wasn't that bad; I just felt a gush of water coming out and all over the bed like I had wet myself. I started to have mild contractions again and with every contraction, more water would gush out. It felt horrible. I just wanted her to change the bed and get it away from me.

My midwife came back from her lunch and put the drip in. She changed my bed and put me on a monitor. I could hear the heartbeat, which really reassured me as I hadn't felt much movement. Literally about five minutes after the drip was in, the most horrendous wave came over my stomach. What I had been feeling all night was not a contraction – *this* was a contraction. A friend who is a midwife had told me that if you do six long, deep breaths, the contraction will be over. I was really focused on doing this, but it was lasting 13 breaths before it was gone.

After three contractions like this, I hit panic mode and I remember tears running down my face. Trudy and the midwife were talking about something, then looked round to see me crying. I said I couldn't do this and I needed an epidural. She said the anaesthetist was in theatre, but as soon as he was out, she would get him.

An hour had passed with these horrific contractions and I couldn't stand it any more. I begged the midwife to let me have a section, but she tried to calm me down and said it didn't quite work like that. She gave me some gas and air to try but after one suck of it, I vomited everywhere. She chased up the anaesthetist and said it would be no more than half an hour. I begged her to stop the drip until he came, which she did. The contractions were still coming every minute, but didn't feel as intense.

I remember looking at the clock; it was 2.30 when the

anaesthetist came in. I've never been so happy to see a man in my whole life. He brought a nurse with him, an older lady with blonde hair. She told me to hold on to her as tight as I needed to stay still. By this point my contractions were off the chart again. I felt so much pressure in my bum and remember saying out loud that I thought my bum was going to burst. I had to wait for the contraction to be over before he could start, but every time he was ready to go, another one would come.

I felt nothing in my back when he was trying to get the needle in. I kept having to stop him with another contraction. Sitting over the side of the bed I could now feel the immense pressure of having to push. No one was listening to me when I said I felt like I was sitting on her head. The anaesthetist was getting really angry at me and shouting to stay still. I remember they lost the baby's heartbeat at one point so my midwife was pushing something into my pelvis, the wee blonde nurse was pulling me forward, the epidural guy was fiddling about my back and I was sitting on one bum cheek trying not to push. I felt totally out of control.

He finally got the epidural in after four or five attempts. I begged my midwife to check me as I was convinced I needed to start pushing. She eventually did and saw that I was 10 cm. She asked Trudy to push the buzzer for another midwife and told me to get ready to start pushing. The pain of the contraction and the pressure to push was overwhelming. I asked if I could blow the pain out. I remember her saying yes, but I wasn't going to be able to blow the baby out.

I tried my hardest not to push, but my body just took over. Every fear I had about pooing myself during this stage had gone out of the window. I felt like I was going to burst with the immense pressure. I saw the midwife clipping on these blue stirrups onto the side of the bed. I tried to say, please don't put my legs in these, but I couldn't get any words out. She told me that I was starting to tear, so they were going to cut me as it would heal. I couldn't have cared less what they did, I just wanted her out.

I heard a clinking of a trolley and saw the other midwife opening a tray covered in blue paper. I saw her lift out scissors, then felt her put her fingers inside me and pull the skin down towards the ground. She waited for the next contraction and then I felt a piercing pain going down through my bum and blood trickled down it. That felt hauntingly familiar. They said the head was out and not to push, just blow. After a final push she was out. A little girl, born at 4.41pm.

They placed her on top of me and I remember thinking, oh this is horrible, she is so slimy and covered in blood. I suddenly felt really dizzy and weak and thought I was going to drop her. I couldn't stop shaking, but they still wouldn't take her off me. I don't really remember delivering the placenta, I just remember being stitched. This was just as sore as the contractions. I could feel it every time the needle pierced my skin.

I needed stitches where I had torn, where they had cut me and where they had put the catheter in. I remember asking the midwife if the stitches were meant to feel as tight as this and she said, 'Can you feel that?' I was like, 'hell yeah I can!' She said I shouldn't be feeling it with the epidural in. I told her I could feel every part of it, I could feel my stomach and would be able to stand up and walk too. She gave me a local anaesthetic for the rest of it. After about half an hour, they gave her to Trudy and I literally vomited everywhere. The nurse gave me a jag to stop the sickness.

I remember phoning my mum during this and saying I needed her to bring the baby's case up now, because she was here. She let out a cry down the phone and was shocked it had come so quickly.

They took her over to weigh her and asked if I had picked a name. She was 7lb 6oz and I knew right away she was a Lucy. ♥

## CHAPTER 8

# Lucy – my whole world

*'You are my angel; you remind me of the goodness in this world and inspire me to be the greatest version of myself.' – Steve Maraboli*

This has been one of the hardest chapters for me to write in the whole book – and one of the easiest. How do you begin to put into words the way you feel about your child? How can I possibly describe the love I have for this little human being? The unconditional love and the bond you have as a parent is indescribable, but when I put together the journey I have been on to have my little miracle, my heart bursts out of my chest every time I think about her.

The decision I took to have Lucy on my own was not an easy one, but it wasn't as hard as you may think. As soon as I had decided I was going to pursue my dreams of trying to be a mum, I knew I would have to put everything aside to make this happen.

Lucy came into this world on the 22$^{nd}$ of April 2014, and that day my life changed forever. It was no longer about me. I had created this amazing little person who was solely reliable on me and I knew I would give everything I had to make sure I did it to the best of my ability. Lucy gave me a whole new perspective on life – good things can happen after all!

The first year of Lucy's life felt reassuringly familiar. I felt the happiest I had ever been. I hadn't remembered feeling like that for a long time. Lucy and I were in a bubble, just her and me for that first year. We created amazing memories with some special friends that will last a lifetime. She made my heart burst everyday with her little smile and her wee cheeky personality. The traits were there from the start – what an incredibly independent, funny and beautiful young girl she would become.

It was not all plain sailing, as any mother knows. The pressures of parenthood are also something you can't describe, and nothing can prepare you for them. But like any mother, I got through it and carried on to the next day. The hard parts were always overridden by the happy times. Having spent my whole pregnancy worrying that something terrible was going to happen, I was enjoying being in the present moment and felt very grateful for every experience I got to have with Lucy – good and bad.

Going it alone as a single parent comes with many challenges. I have nothing to compare it to, so I didn't, and still don't feel hard done to that I was juggling everything on my own. I will say though that I don't think I could do it without the support of my parents. My mum and dad have been and continue to be one of the biggest parts of Lucy's life since the day she was born and have helped me out immeasurably with raising her. One of the most positive (and scariest) things about being a single parent is that you are responsible for the upbringing of this little person you have created. I am the one who makes all of the decisions for Lucy, I don't have to argue with anyone, I don't have to negotiate anything with another parent, and I don't need to worry about any in laws! (Going it alone can have its advantages.)

I do worry about what this means for Lucy though. I constantly worry if I am enough for her. Will she resent me for not having a dad? Will she feel that she has lost out on not having another side to her family? I know I have all of this to come with Lucy, as she is still only seven and doesn't really have any understanding of this. She has asked questions in the past about why she doesn't have a dad and I've told her that mummy couldn't find a nice enough daddy for her, so a doctor helped to put her in my tummy.

I remember the first time Lucy mentioned anything about a daddy. When she was two years old, we were driving along the boulevard and a taxi was driving alongside us. She looked out the window and said 'daddy?' I quickly said, 'That's not Lucy's daddy, Lucy doesn't have a daddy.' That was the first time I had really thought about it and how I was going to explain this to her in the future. When she was really little, I used the narrative that 'Lucy doesn't have a daddy, she has a Granda and an Uncle Graham who love her more than a daddy.' She happily accepted this and if any of her friends asked, she would innocently say, 'I don't have a daddy'.

As she has got older and started primary school, she has

become more aware of this and sees lots of her friends doing things with their dads. I often feel pangs of guilt that I have been selfish in denying her a father. I am very open with Lucy and often ask her if she has any questions about not having a dad. She will at times say that she wishes she had a dad, and I acknowledge and validate her feelings with this. We always get back to the fact that she and I are a team and it will be the two of us forever.

As for what the future hold with this one, I have no idea and I am probably in no way prepared for it, but all I know is that I love her more than life and will do anything to make sure she has the best life possible.

This amazing little girl has taught me how to live again. She has shown me a love that I never knew possible, she has taught me lessons I never thought I would have to face and she has reignited a fire inside me and a determination to fight till the day I die to make sure what happened to me does not define me. I just hope one day that she will look back on this journey and see how much she was wanted and is loved and will be proud of me for what I had to overcome to have her.

CHAPTER 9

# Triggered back into therapy

*'It comes back. It always comes back – the things you didn't deal with, those feeling you didn't sort out. You can go years and years without thinking about it and then one day, out of the blue, it taps you on the shoulder and says, Oh hey, remember me?'*
*– Kristin Kory*

The first three years of Lucy's life were an absolute dream. I was living in the bubble of what could be described as a 'normal' parenthood. This came with its own stresses and strains, but for the first time, these three years were about Lucy and me, nothing to do with what had happened to me.

This all changed in April 2017, when a baby from my nursery was badly injured and ended up on life support in intensive care. An attempted murder charge was brought upon the two people who were living with him. Our whole staff team were devastated and could not process the fact that someone could hurt an innocent little baby in this way.

The little boy was the same age as Lucy. I could not

comprehend anyone harming a child in that way. What I didn't expect to resurface was lots of buried memories from my own trauma. At that point, I had not acknowledged the fact that what had happened to me was also in fact attempted murder; I only found this out later on in therapy. My body seemed to resonate with this long before I had any memories or words to articulate it.

I was summoned to court as a witness for this little boy, which began to play tricks with my mind. I started to believe that I was going to court for my own trial and that when I got there, I would be giving evidence against the two men that raped me. Lots of fears that I had buried after having Lucy quickly resurfaced and my thinking became very irrational again. I now know that this was all a symptom of PTSD and the resurfacing of memories that I had never faced.

This triggered me back into therapy. I was so reluctant to try and tell my story to someone else as I had felt such a loss with Irene, my carer who died. I knew if I was going to go anywhere, it would be back to the CARA project. In December 2017, I met with Karen Laing. Initially when I asked her for help, I thought I would only need a few sessions to get through the court case and move on from it. I don't think Karen quite knew what she was letting herself in for when she agreed to help me.

This was the start of another powerful relationship, and one that has been key to my healing journey. I immediately felt the same connection with Karen that I had with Irene. I didn't think that would be possible and I almost felt guilty for clicking with Karen so quickly, as if she were replacing Irene. Guilt was such a familiar emotion to me and has been one of the hardest ones to break in my journey through therapy.

Like Irene, Karen never pushed me into anything I wasn't ready for. By this point, I felt I was more ready to speak about some of the detail, although I had no idea of the depth of detail that I had disassociated from. This is where I learned about disassociation. Karen explained to me how my brain had disconnected from the event in order to survive and whilst that was needed back then, it was not what I needed now. I was in a space where I was ready to address the memories, process them and let them go. This seems so much easier than it sounds and I had no idea of the journey that was ahead of me to let it go.

As I started to work through my story with Karen, she very quickly identified my habit of avoidance in certain areas. Karen never pushed me to tell my story, but there was something burning inside me that made me feel I had to put it all together to finally be able to let it go. She used different techniques to support me, finding words for my thoughts. Karen was the first person to say to me that she felt I had CPTSD – complex post-traumatic stress disorder. Talking through a diagnosis like this made me feel quite relieved that there were actual words and symptoms for what I was feeling, and that I was not simply going crazy.

It was at this point that I felt a deeper connection with Karen and allowed myself to start opening up to her on a different level. I told her how suicidal I felt, things that I had done in the past and how I was coping day to day. Karen never once judged me or made me feel bad about myself. I was terrified that if I was honest they would take Lucy away from me, or I would end up in hospital. Karen again reassured me that this was all symptoms of trauma and a completely normal response.

I knew I was going to a different level in this therapy process when my body started remembering things that I had not found words for. Karen explained this as 'somatic experiencing'. This is where the scars of past trauma go beyond the physical injury and emotional pain and manifest themselves in a range of different symptoms. I could taste blood in my mouth, I began to feel pains in my thighs and shooting pains through my vagina. I felt like I was choking and could not breathe. I could not understand how I was experiencing this pain 16 years after it had happened, yet it felt familiar.

I remember during one session, Karen asked me where was I when I could taste the blood – was I lying on my front or on my back, how did I know it was blood, was it his penis or his fingers, how did I know this? I was able to answer all her questions and put together pieces of information that were flying around inside my brain. This was the first time I had been able to do this. Karen said that she observed my body going into shock, so she stopped at this point and brought me back into the room. I felt like I was right back in that memory, I could feel things, I could hear things, I could taste things. I truly thought I was going insane.

Hard as these sessions were, they soon became my safe place where I could be fully honest with someone about how I was feeling, where my head was at and how I was coping. Karen offered me so much comfort, and she was the first person I allowed to properly comfort me when I broke down. Karen would tell me this was what I needed to do back then, but because I had disassociated, I never got the opportunity. Sometimes Karen would just hold me in her arms as I melted into a puddle, crying uncontrollably. I finally felt safe to do this. My body felt safe and my mind felt safe. Karen said she could feel my whole body let go when she did this. I had no idea how much my body was bracing itself for danger. Every muscle was clenched, especially in the lower half of my body.

We talked through things that could have been linked with the physical and emotional pain over the years. This included reoccurring urine infections, thrush in my mouth, pain in my pelvic area – all of which I never acknowledged to be part of what happened. Reflecting on this I can now see that this may have been my body's way of trying to get my mind to address what happened, but I never did.

Karen made me see how I was reinforcing certain thoughts in my mind by repeating behaviours, i.e., every time I woke up from a nightmare, I had to check the bed for blood. We worked through strategies to try and change my mindset to reassure my body and mind that this was not happening in the present moment. I also told her that I had carried a pair of pants in my bag ever since this had happened. In my mind, this was so that I was prepared if it would happen again that I wouldn't have to tie pants together to stop the blood. Karen made me see that I was preparing in my mind for it to happen again, even if it was subconsciously. It took me a long time to be able to stop doing this, but it highlighted what a hold it had over me.

Karen identified a disconnect between the person I had been when it had happened to the person I was now. I thought of these people as two different people, when in reality they were both me. I hated 'that person' for what had happened that night. I blamed 'that person' for leaving herself, for ruining my life. I never once blamed the people that carried out the attack on my body and mind. I saw 'this' person as the one whose body was contaminated, the one who had so many dark thoughts, the one who couldn't process the memories, who was 'failing' to move on and let it go.

We spoke about my feelings towards the two men who had raped me, and never once had I felt any feelings of anger towards them. We worked out that fear was my dominating emotion when it came to thoughts and memories, and I could not get past the fear to feel any anger. Any anger I felt was directed inwardly, which was the safer option in my head.

There were many times when I felt that I was so deeply stuck in my trauma that I would never get to the other side. Feeling stuck has been something I have felt throughout this whole healing journey, yet every time I have made it out. It's only when you take a step back that you are able to see all the little things that you have overcome, which are actually quite huge in reality.

Karen had managed to get me to a deeper place of working through my trauma than I had ever been before. I had begun to understand disassociation, PTSD, the impact of trauma on the brain and why my body was feeling pain now that had almost been frozen in time, but I still had not 'worked out' how to let it go.

Sadly, my working relationship with Karen came to an abrupt end as she had to take time off for personal reasons. We were not able to resume the working relationship we had, which left me feeling lost and as if my world was in disarray again. I felt another sense of loss, similar to that I had felt with Irene. My irrational thoughts told me that it was my fault that Karen had to go off sick and that my trauma was too complicated for her or anyone to manage. I of course know this not to be true!

Karen was one of those people who come into your life when you need them most. I will never be able to find the right words to tell her how much she means to me and how grateful I am for everything she did for me.

CHAPTER 10

# Finding mindfulness

*'Connection – The energy that exists between people when they feel seen, heard and valued, when they can give and receive without judgement; and when they derive sustenance and strength from the relationship' – Brene Brown*

I have been lucky enough to meet some amazing people on my journey towards healing. Just before my relationship with Karen ended, I had started a mindfulness course in a bid to try some alternative methods to complement my therapy with Karen, all in an attempt to let go. In December 2018, another Karen, the friend who I had been on the night of the attack, who knew how much I had been struggling, suggested that we should try a mindfulness course. I was dubious at first as I didn't like meeting new people and didn't know if I would have to speak in front of anyone. However I decided I had nothing to lose, so I would give it a go.

We arrived at a converted church venue in Rutherglen called No. 18. When we walked into the room, I remember looking at the facilitator and thinking, *she's a lot younger than I thought she would be.* Lee was about my age and had amazing taste in clothes (first impressions and all that!) She was the facilitator of the course and radiated an air of kindness, genuineness and warmth. I immediately thought – 'I like her'! I don't often say that about people I meet for the first time, but this was where the universe led me to Lee. She was the person who was going to see me through the next part of my journey, and she would never know how much she has done for me and how much space she holds in my heart.

The mindfulness course gave me many new strategies to help me try to move on from living in the past. I learned more about breathing techniques, unhelpful thinking patterns (thoughts train), being more in the present moment and doing things that made your heart sing. It was here that I uncovered a new-found love of nature and being in the outdoors. I was always teased by my friends and colleagues for not being an 'outdoor person', never wearing wellies unless they matched my hat and scarf, horrified if I got a bit of dirt on me, moaning if I got wet and always saying I was freezing. Yet these were all the things that I now began to love. I loved being out in the fresh air, feeling the cold on my face. I didn't mind being out in the rain; there was something cathartic about it, watching it run down my jacket, as if washing something away. Nature soon became a place I would go to regain a sense of calm.

I took something away from all of the sessions that I attended on the course, but the last one was particularly special. It was about letting go. We had to share something with the group that we wanted to let go of. This was an extremely powerful and emotional session for everyone in the group as we all tried to let go of some demons.

This had been a very powerful for journey for Karen and me, but as the sessions went on, I realised that she had been carrying something heavy that I had no idea about. She had carried a lot of guilt for what had happened to me, feeling that she was responsible for letting me go on my own. I couldn't believe she had carried this all these years and I had known nothing about it. We had never really spoken about it after it happened, and now I knew why. That night I felt I had helped Karen to let go of the guilt that she was wrongly holding on to, just as I was. We both shared with the circle in what was one of the scariest but powerful most feelings I had experienced. I didn't go into detail, I simply said that it was time for me to let go of a lot of guilt and shame I was holding onto that was not mine to carry. I think I thought by saying this out loud, it might help me let go there and then, but unfortunately it is not as easy as that. However, I had planted that seed and put an intention out there, which made me realise that this was my time to go hard or go home. Now was the time I had to work harder than ever, because I no longer wanted the hurt and the pain to continue taking over my life.

When Karen went off sick, I quickly knew that I could not do this on my own. I had come so far with her and if I put it all back in the box, the last two years would have been a waste. I quietly had a feeling about Lee that she could be the person to help me get to the end of this journey. (Again, I talk about 'the end' as if there is one – I now know it was just a place in my mind that does not exist.) I reached out to Lee to see if she could help me on a 1:1 basis. Lee agreed to do 1:1 coaching with me and this was another relationship that would take me further than I had ever been.

I don't remember this, but Lee said that on my first session with her, I told her that I had been gang raped. I had never opened up to someone that quickly and most definitely I had never said 'that word' so openly. That was one of the few times when I did use the word 'rape' with Lee. Both Karen and Irene had already highlighted to me that I wasn't using the correct term for what happened, and any time they mentioned it, I would look away in shame. Lee kindly guided me into exploring what this word meant to me and helped me to see that I never wanted to acknowledge the reality of its meaning, which was one of the biggest hindrances in me accepting what had happened. Until I had accepted it, I could not let go and move on.

Lee and I initially saw each other monthly, then progressed to weekly. The commitment that Lee gave me in helping me get 'to the end' was something I can never thank her enough for. As she tried to juggle her own working life, her family life and being a part-time coach, she blew my brain as to how she managed to fit it all in, ultimately to the detriment of herself. But Lee had made a commitment to me that she would help me get to the end of my story, then work on moving on, which she did.

Like Karen, Lee would never be fazed by anything I told her.

She was always immensely supportive, caring, compassionate and kind. She too would pick me up off the floor when I fainted, come to the toilet with me when I felt I was going to be sick and hold me and reassure me until my body came back to safety again. The relationship I had and continue to have with Lee is like to no other. She opened so many doors for me and introduced me to many paths that would take me on different directions in this journey.

## CHAPTER 11

# Madeleine Black

*'A hero is one who heals their own wounds and then shows others how to do the same.' – Yung Pueblo*

During a session I had with Lee on the 25th of July 2019, she introduced me to a TED Talk (TED talks are short video presentations) by an incredible lady called Madeleine Black. Little did she know then what an impact this video would have on my recovery and healing journey.

Madeleine spoke about her experience of being gang-raped at 13. Her talk blew my mind, so many were the common factors in our stories. Something connected deep inside when I heard her speak. She gave me words for memories I could not articulate and shared emotions that felt so raw and real for me. I felt like she was inside my brain and could see into my soul (even though she had no idea who I was).

My heart ached for Madeleine when I heard her story. I cried and felt gut-wrenchingly sad for her. The pain she must have been in, the fear she would be feeling, the way she left her body at times. These feelings resonated so much with me, as they were all I had known for such a long time. I finally felt that someone knew exactly what I had been through I and I wasn't crazy or going insane after all.

The sadness I felt was overwhelming, but these feelings were for Madeleine – I would not allow myself to feel any of this for myself. I could not allow myself to accept that what had happened to Madeleine had in fact happened to me too. I was in awe of her strength, how she could speak so openly and honestly about her experience and use it in a way to help others. I still couldn't even say the word that described what happened to me, never mind share my story to help others, yet I got a feeling inside that this was something I had to do.

After watching Madeleine's TED Talk, I immediately bought her book, titled *Unbroken.* Knowing that Madeleine had got to a place where she could move on with her life gave me some hope that I might be able to do this too.

Her book was even more harrowing and inspiring than her talk. I desperately read through the chapters to see how she had managed to get to the place she was in now. All these years I had wished for someone to tell me how to get over what had happened. Madeleine gave a step-by-step account of her journey and how she got to where she is today. But this was Madeleine's journey and I have learned over this process that each person's journey is completely unique to them and there is no 'guide to' how to overcome trauma.

Having watched the TED Talk and read her book, I felt a

new sense of determination to get moving from the place I was in. Lee's support in this was instrumental in helping me get to where I wanted to go. She never pushed me into something I didn't want to do. She sometimes gave me a nudge, but was always super-respectful of my boundaries, whilst supporting me through the difficult parts.

Through my whole healing journey, I wanted to be able to piece together my story and put it down on paper. So many fragments had been flying about in my head for so long and I felt that only by piecing them together would I be able to fully let go of what happened. I wanted to take control, I wanted to do this for me.

Lee and I worked very intensely over a few sessions and from that point, I was able to write my story in full. Memories came back to me of things that I had no idea had happened. I realised out that I hadn't been raped twice, it had in fact been five times. I experienced pain that I had no idea you could feel when it wasn't happening in the present. I doubted my sanity on many occasions and was convinced that if anyone had heard what we talked about in our sessions, I would have been carted off to hospital.

However, I did it. It was an extremely hard and excruciating thing to do, but I did it. I finally achieved something that I had wanted to do for such a long time. I was taking my power back.

CHAPTER 12

# The full story of that night

*'Tragedies do happen. We can discover the reason, blame others, imagine how different our lives would be had they not occurred. But none of that is important; they did occur, and so be it. From there onward we must put aside the fear that they awoke in us and begin to rebuild.' – Paula Coelho.*

25th January 2003

WARNING – this chapter contains explicit detail.

So here goes…

It has taken me nearly 18 years to get this story out, both in my head and on paper. These are memories I had buried away so deeply that I didn't know they existed. I have had to endure many flashbacks, much physical pain and debilitating fear in reliving all of this, but I'm now in a place where I need to own my story. I need to accept what happened, find strength in what I have endured and survived and hopefully, one day, use this to help others.

On Saturday the 25th of January (Burns Night) 2003, I was out for the night celebrating Karen's 21st birthday. The night started off full of laughter and fun, with us thinking we were movie stars riding into town in a limo, but it ended very differently.

Upon leaving the nightclub we had been in, I remember crossing the road and walking down Queen Street. Debenhams was right in front of me, so I knew the taxi rank was right underneath it. Out of nowhere, I felt an overwhelming sense that there was someone behind me. Before I had a chance to look round, I felt a hand come over my mouth and nose and felt myself being lifted off the ground. I don't have much recollection of how I came to be at the end of this lane, just off Queen Street. Everything was so dark and I very quickly had been overcome with panic and fear. I had no idea what was happening or what was about to happen.

The next memory is of being pushed against the wall face first. My cheek was pressing so hard into the brick that I thought it was going to go through it. I could even taste brick in my mouth, if that is possible. I still had no clue what was happening – if I was being robbed, if I was about to be killed. Maybe it was my innocence and naivety at that time, but what was about to happen had not entered my thoughts – yet.

I then felt my skirt being pulled up from behind. This was where the realisation hit me of what my attacker was trying to do, and I completely panicked. I could feel him pull my pants so hard that they ripped off at one side. This is the last point when I have any memory of having pants on. I don't remember how they came to be fully off and end up where they did.

I could feel the whole weight of his body pushing against mine and further into the wall. I could then feel his skin on my skin, even down to the hairs on his legs. I had no idea how or when he got his trousers down. I could then feel his hand around my buttocks and knowing what he was about to do, I tried to scream for help.

I could hear myself screaming in my head, but nothing would come out my mouth – it was like my voice box had been disabled. I could then feel something hard pressing against my buttocks. Naively I didn't know what it was at first, but then I realised it was his penis, which he was trying to force inside me. Somehow I managed to clench tight to try and stop this from happening, but this just made him angry. Although I still couldn't see anything, I could feel his aggression from behind as he kicked my right leg open with force. As he did that, I fell off my heels and had a shooting pain go through my ankle which was quickly replaced by an indescribable burning, piercing, tearing pain shoot right through my back passage. I felt like I had been torn in half.

He must have been inside for only seconds when I managed to push him off me. I don't know what I thought I was going to do when I did this as I couldn't move any of my body, it felt like it had frozen and still no words would come out. This only angered him more – he punched me in the stomach and I fell to the ground. It took me 17 years to realise (and accept) that this had been anal rape.

This was the one and only time I was able to offer any fight back. I beat myself up for years about this, thinking that if I had done more, I could have stopped it. I know now that nothing would have stopped what was happening that night and when I did try, it felt like it only made the situation worse.

I don't know how I got to be lying on my back after he punched me in the stomach, but I remember lying there with nothing on my bottom half. Time almost seemed to stand still at points and this was one of them. The images in my head were still very much of darkness at this stage. I had no memory of seeing his face at this point or what he was wearing. I think I was probably in shock and unable to process what had happened, from me leaving to get the taxi to now.

I remember him saying that this was all my doing and I had asked for it, but I couldn't understand what I had done. Had he seen me in the nightclub, had I done something to suggest I wanted this? I now know that this was his way of justifying what he was doing and in fact it was nothing to do with me. It had nothing to do with what I was wearing or anything I had done. 100% of all rapes are by rapists – it has nothing to do with the victims. It has taken me a long time to get to see this point of view as I had been so deeply conditioned into believing the things that were said to me that night and it has only been with a lot of work that I have been able to start to shift my own thinking.

Then, out of nowhere, I was aware of another person behind me to my left – another man. For a split second I felt relief that someone was here to rescue me, that I was safe and that he would make sure I wasn't hurt any more. That was very quickly overtaken again by a fear that can't be described in words. The extremes of emotions that I felt in those few seconds are very much a reflection of how I have navigated my way through this journey – opposite feelings that can flip so quickly that you can't describe it.

As the realisation hit that this man was not here to save me, I could feel him pull my hands behind my head and hold me down by the shoulders. The first man started to move his hand down my thighs to open my legs. I then felt the most horrific stabbing pain shoot through my vagina. I don't know if I let out a scream, but his hands quickly went over my mouth and I could taste the blood on his fingers. I remember digging my nails into my hands to try and focus on a different pain, but nothing would take it away.

For all these years, I thought he had pushed his fingers inside me, but after a series of flashbacks working through this story with Lee, I now know it wasn't his fingers. I have an image in my head of his arm in a forward motion coming towards me and then this memory of something piercingly sharp. At one point I was not sure if this had been a knife or a broken bottle, but I now know that it was a knife. It was just a small pen knife that you can flick open, but it made so much sense that this was had caused the pain and not his fingers. Although I say it was small, that does not take away the magnitude of being stabbed, especially in that area.

For years I have had a fixation on the question of how much blood I lost that night, and whilst I do not know the full extent of the damage that can be caused by rape, I just felt that it wouldn't have caused that much blood loss. This memory made so much sense to me and helped me understand another piece of the jigsaw.

As I said earlier, I feel that for some parts of that night, time stood still, and this was one of those moments. As I was experiencing this sharp shooting pain, the second man behind me stubbed his cigarette out on my chest, in between my breasts. I have a vivid memory of seeing his hands come over my head with a small cigarette in between his fingers. I have no idea how my memory can be so vivid with this, as the place was pitch black, but I can see this so clearly. I could see what he was doing and could smell the smoke, but I felt nothing, and I still have no memory of any pain in that area from the cigarette burns.

I then began to feel the first man move his body on top of mine. His whole weight was on top of me, and I could hardly catch a breath. There was a slight space at the top of my chest which wasn't pinned down by his weight and that's the bit I could breathe from. I could feel his legs forcing my thighs apart again and his erect penis trying to go inside me. I could feel him pushing against me to get inside, but it seemed that it wouldn't fit. He tried again and this time, it felt like his whole weight had gone through my body. I thought he had torn right through my vagina and back passage together. This was the point when I remember opening my eyes and getting the first glimpse of his face. I have associated what visual memory I have of his face with this point – the point when I opened my eyes, when he pushed his body into mine. I have avoided any memories of his face as I associated his face with that pain.

I don't know how I survived this pain; it was something that words will never be able to describe. I thought I was going to be sick, but that brought me back to the feelings of terror that if I angered him, it would get worse. I swallowed my vomit in a bid to not anger him any more.

The memories I have of him are that he was of medium build with dark, short hair and sallow skin. He did not have any piercings or tattoos that were visible. His eyes were beady and almost evil looking. His eyes are what haunt me most.

As he was forcing himself inside me, I could hear the other man telling him to 'do it harder'. I felt like my whole body was shaking uncontrollably. I'm not sure if this was due to the cold, his violent movements or shock setting in, but I started to feel very dizzy at this point and am unsure if I went in and out of consciousness with the pain. I kept trying to get a breath, but every time I would exhale to try and get another breath, I would feel the sharp shooting feeling travel further up inside me.

Feeling dizzy as I did with varying levels of consciousness, my memories of the whole experience are blurred, and I still have lots of blanks and gaps that must be the result of having passed out periodically. Today, feeling dizzy is a trigger for losing control and feeling pain. It has also been a coping strategy that during therapy I have been trying to stop using, because when I am trying to work through aspects of this night and things get too much for me, I faint.

The moments I describe as going out of my body are exactly that – I could no longer feel any of what was going on inside me and I remember focusing on the weirdest thing. There was a set of council industrial bins down that lane (any sight of bins like that still haunts me). I remember trying to focus on these bins and the writing on them through my left eye. It said 'Glasgow City Council' and they were a bottle-green colour. I remember randomly trying to make up different words with the letters on the bins – 'glow', 'go', 'goal', 'saw'. This seemed to take me away from what was happening.

I also have a vision of physically being out of my body and looking down on myself from the building up above. I can feel myself sitting on top of the roof, watching what was happening to my body. The man on top of me had a black shirt and dark denims on, which he had pulled down past his knees. I have no clue how I would have this vision of his clothes, as I was underneath and I was very aware of keeping my eyes shut for most of it.

I remember the point I came back into my body, and that was when the second man moved round to the left side of my head. He must have let my arms go to be in this position, but I still had no control over my body whatsoever and couldn't have moved even if I had wanted to. I snapped back into my body, and heard the piercing sound of his zip in my ear. I couldn't understand or process why I would be hearing this sound as his penis was already inside me. As I turned my eyes to the left to see what it was, my right cheek was pulled around where my gaze was met by what seemed like another huge penis.

Again, before I had time to take in what was happening, something hit the back of my throat. I couldn't breathe – my whole airway was blocked. I could feel myself gagging, but I was trying so hard not to be sick in case I angered them more. I'm not sure if I was sick or not, I just remember this overwhelming feeling of gagging, which I still struggle with to this day. I could feel a persistent banging at the back of my throat. I remember thinking that if I could try and bite down hard I might be able to stop this, but it was like my brain was not getting this message through to my body, and my mouth was paralysed. I remember him coming inside my mouth and the fluid going everywhere. I could taste it like chalk and salt mixed together, running down my cheeks, in between my teeth, even coming out my nose. I could not spit or manage to get any of it out my mouth, it just felt like it was everywhere. As I lay there with the other man violating my body down below, I heard him telling me I was vile and disgusting.

I felt trapped inside a body that couldn't move – couldn't do anything. My head was screaming 'please someone help me', but no words would come out of my mouth. It was at the point when all this was happening to me that I feel I left my body again. I remember wondering if I was going to die, what would my mum and dad do, who would find my body, or would anyone find it at all. I remember a feeling of nothingness.

I don't know at what point it was 'over', but the banging inside me had stopped, and I heard him saying how useless I had been as I 'hadn't even made him come'. I remember feeling like I was lying in a puddle, but they weren't his body fluids, they were mine, and only when I got up and touched myself, did I know the puddle was blood.

I'm not clear which of them said this, but one of them told me that if I moved from there, they would come back and do it all again. I could hear them walking away laughing. To this day, I don't know how long I waited for. I don't remember finding any of my clothes, I just remember trying to move, but thinking I was going to pass out from the pain. I could see the end of the lane and I remember thinking that if I could just get to the end of it, someone would see me and I could get help.

I got myself up and started walking towards the end of the lane. I remember getting to the bin that I had been focusing on, thinking that was me nearly there, and then all of a sudden, I felt my heart just stop. A face emerged from behind the bin. At that point I believed my life was over. I had not listened to what they had said and any chance of getting to safety had just disappeared.

I don't know how I got back to where we had been, but I remember lying back on the ground. I have a sense of my being quite submissive during this part and actually laying myself on the ground and allowing my body to take what was about to happen. I have struggled with a lot of guilt and shame regarding this – how could I just allow myself to get into a position to allow the same thing to happen again?

Working through it, I am starting to accept that I was trying to protect myself in a crazy way from making the situation worse, which I believed I had already done by not listening to what they had said in the first place. I felt that same sharp, excruciating pain of his penis being forced back inside me. This was a new level of pain. Again, I have only recently recovered memories of this. The pain I was feeling was not from vaginal rape, this was another attempt at anal rape, and this time he managed to follow through with it. I felt my legs being pushed so far back, almost up to my chin, that it obstructed my airway again. At this point I feel like I left my body again, as I began to feel nothing. I have this vision again of what was happening to me from up above, sitting on top of the roof. This time the guy had a white shirt and black jeans.

I now felt at peace, believing that I was simply going to die. I wasn't scared any more, I just wanted it to be over, and if dying was the only way that would happen, I was ok with that. I just knew that my body could not take any more and I was happy to let go.

I remember coming back into my body and feeling the banging feeling again. Somehow, he had managed to move from being inside me anally to my vagina. Although I was back in my body, I could no longer feel anything. I felt like I was in a parallel universe and had completely disconnected from the person I was.

And then it was over. I still had that feeling of nothingness. I could feel body fluids all over me – running down my legs, on my abdomen, down my hips – just everywhere. He softly said in my ear that if I told anyone no one would believe me, and if

I did, he would find me, do it again and finish the job this time. That quiet whisper has echoed in my ear and I can feel my head pull away to the side every time I think of it. These words have shaped a large part of my trauma experience and the decisions I have made ever since. They warned me once before and I didn't listen, so this time I had every reason to believe he was telling the truth and would follow through with his threats.

The guilt and shame had already started to envelope my body and my mind. Nothing was ever going to be the same again.

I don't remember him leaving or how long I waited to leave. I remember a sense of almost waking up and having an overwhelming urge to move, get my clothes and go. My pants were on the other side of the wall, where they had originally been ripped off. I could feel the blood and semen running down my legs, and knew I had to stop it. At this point I knew that it was no longer about getting out of the lane to get help, it was about getting home and getting back to 'normal'. I had to make this not have happened. No one could know, or I would face the threat of it happening all over again.

I remember having napkins in my bag that I pushed inside me to stop the bleeding. I tied my pants back together and started walking towards the end of the lane as quickly as I could. I didn't even look at the bin on the way past; I almost feel like I floated to the end of that lane, and I still don't know how I did it, but I made it to the end. I could see people, I could see lights and I could see the Debenhams sign again. At that point, I knew I was going home.

Little did I know that hardest part of the journey was still to come.

That night stole many things that can never be brought back. It stole my virginity, my innocence, my sense of safety, my self-worth, my soul.

CHAPTER 13

# Remembering: the aftermath

*'Progress through something traumatic, it's not linear. It's not like we go from unhealthy to unhealthy, failure to success. I think it's all circular. You just back around to the same pain and the same loneliness. But each time you come around, you're stronger from the climb.'* – Glennon Doyle Melton

The days and weeks after getting my story out and put on paper were extremely difficult. I could not believe I had managed to do it. Now that I had, was I not supposed to have let it go? This is what I had always thought would have happened and then I would be able to move on.

Sadly, that wasn't the case. I now had to come to terms with the magnitude of what happened. I had to come to terms with the fact that I had in fact been raped four times and that what had happened was in fact attempted murder. How do you begin to process that?

They say healing is about letting go, acknowledging the trauma and accepting that it happened. It doesn't mean that you have to make peace with it, it doesn't mean you have to forgive, it doesn't mean that you will ever get over it and it doesn't mean that it will ever go away.

Those three little words 'let it go' sound so simple, but on this journey they have felt so impossible and so out of reach. I constantly asked myself, why can't you just let it go? But that as confusing as asking what the colour yellow smells like. It has turned into a battle of self-hatred as I felt this was something else I was incapable of achieving.

Now that I had managed to get my story out, it was time to learn how to live again, how to deconstruct all of the negative thought patterns and habits that I had created as a means to survive. The only way I could let go was by trying to live again, and by that I mean live authentically as the person I am now. The person I was back then no longer exists, but that person was not to blame for what happened. I had to find a way to forgive myself, to allow my worlds to connect and find out who I really was.

## CHAPTER 14

# Telling my parents, at last

*'There's no greater agony than bearing an untold story inside you.' – Maya Angelou*

The work I had been carrying out with Lee had allowed me to see how hard it was to let go whilst I still lived with a secret in my own home. This added to the shame and the guilt I felt which were never mine to own. I could not find out who I authentically was whilst I was living two separate lives. The 'me' who would present herself to the world as a happy, caring, kind person, who liked to do things for others, and the 'me' who was overshadowed by the traumatic events of one night.

Lee had never once put pressure on me to tell my parents, but we had explored what that would look like. I began to feel more pressure about lying to them about where I was going every Thursday night and had started to let little thoughts trickle into my mind about what it might mean not to have this secret hanging over me.

Many people have questioned me through the years as to

why I hadn't told my mum and dad. I would get looks of shock and disbelief that I could keep a secret like that to myself. No one who has not been put in that position could understand the reasons why people make decisions after experiencing trauma.

When I managed to escape that lane, I had my attackers' words implanted in my ears that if I told anyone they would find me and kill me. This sounds absurd to anyone looking in from the outside – how would they know where I lived, how would they know if I had told anyone? But with so much adrenaline and cortisol flooding your brain, rational thinking is not possible. If I did tell them, would they believe me? Would they think it was my fault for leaving on my own? If they did believe me, would they make me go to the police? Another part of my thinking was that I didn't want to cause them any pain, and I knew the thought of anything bad happening to their daughter would have devastated them. I wasn't sure that I could cope with their hurt as well as my own.

If I am being really honest with myself, I now know the main reason I didn't tell them is because I didn't want it to be real. I didn't want it to be alive in my home and amongst my family. I didn't want people to feel sorry for me, because at that time I felt I didn't deserve it. I didn't want people to ask me how I was all the time, or worry about me. I just wanted the whole thing to disappear and for things to be the way they were before I went out that night.

I don't remember what made me do it, but I was driving home from a session with Lee when I had an overwhelming urge to just tell my mum and dad, to finally be rid of the horrible dirty secret I had created in my mind. I didn't tell anyone I was going to do it, I hadn't planned it – I just went home and decided to go for it.

I felt ill inside at the thought of saying those words out loud, at the thought of the eruption of pain that was going to spill over into my house. But I had remembered everything that Karen, Lee and Madeleine had said. It was not me who had caused this pain, it was not me who caused the hurt, and if I was ever going to start to get rid of the shame in a bid to forgive myself, I had to start acknowledging this.

As I went into the living room, my mum and dad were both sitting on the couch. I knew this would be the last time I would look at them without seeing immeasurable pain and hurt. I told them I had something to tell them and their body actions changed.

I said that something had happened to me a long time ago and I needed to share it with them to be able to move on. I said the words: I said that I had been raped on a night out, but reassured them that I was ok and I was getting help to move on.

The look of shock and hurt on their faces will haunt me forever. What had I just done to them? They were understandably devastated, crying and in a state of disbelief. I explained that all the nights I had been out was me seeing Lee in a bid to try and move on from the past. I think they were hurt and even a bit angry that I hadn't told them. I knew it was going to take time for them to process it, so I left the wreckage of the grenade I had just thrown into the room and went upstairs. I hadn't told them any detail, but said if they wanted to ask me anything, I would try and answer it.

The ripples from their devastation flooded my house for weeks on end. I felt that my dad could hardly look at me, but I know that's because he wouldn't have been able to handle the thought of two men doing that to me. My poor mum tried to carry on like I hadn't just dropped this massive bomb. She told me if I needed anything that she was there, but was glad that I had Lee to talk to and help me more than she ever could. My mum has never really been an openly emotional person, so I knew she would have buried the hurt way deeper than she would ever let on.

My dad asked if he should tell my family. I said yes, it was fine to do that as I no longer wanted to keep this secret, it wasn't mine any more, but I did not want to talk about it with any of them. I received texts from my aunts and uncles, sharing their devastation, but saying how incredibly proud of me they were. I felt that old familiar enemy of guilt trying to bury itself back into my brain, guilt that all these people in my family were so sad and upset for me, but I worked hard to rationalise this guilt, knowing it was not mine.

I didn't feel the overwhelming sense of relief that people had said I would feel after sharing this secret. It was what it was. I did feel a little lighter knowing that I did not have to make up lies about where I was going any more and my mum and dad were more than supportive in helping me with Lucy to allow me to do what I needed to do.

Although I did not feel it at the time, I now believe that this was the start of me beginning to work towards acceptance. I don't often talk about what happened at home, but I now know that I can if I want too. I know my mum and dad, and in fact my whole family, have a better understanding of me and why I have chosen certain paths in my life, including having Lucy on my own, and it makes sense to them now. I still believe that I did what I had to do at the time to survive and part of that was not telling anyone, but now that I have, it has helped me work towards finding me again.

CHAPTER 15

# 2020 – not another decade

*'Change the way you look at things and the things you look at change.'* – Wayne W Dyer

Lee and I had done lots of work to get to a place where I felt strong enough to make the decision that I would not waste another decade of my life being controlled by what had happened to me. Two decades and 17 years had been long enough. I had left 'the secret' behind me in 2019 and I was heading into 2020 with a fresh mindset. I started the year off with some intentions which I put out to the universe. I no longer wanted to be the victim in my story; I wanted to use it to help others. I would do more of what I loved and what made my heart sing. I would practise gratitude for everything I had in my life and enjoy every minute of my biggest blessing – Lucy. I would no longer be controlled by my fears. Instead, I would face them and smash them, choosing love over fear.

Finally, I would start to find my self-worth again, start to find me. The person I was before that night, the person I was now, the person I had always been, the person who had been buried so deep inside that I had lost her. At the time, I had no idea how I was going to achieve any of this, but there was something about entering a new decade that made me feel empowered to push forward and try something new.

I was given an opportunity very quickly as we entered the new decade. My close friends Kirsty and Gary were due to get married in October 2020, but they had decided to bring their date forward to the 25th of January. That date had shuddered through my bones whenever I had heard it, seen it, or had anything to do with it. Every year I dreaded this day, feeling sick to my core, reliving moments in time and wishing they would pause so I could go back and change the ending. I couldn't believe this was the day my friends chose to get married. How could I possibly celebrate on this date, the date that ruined my life? I toiled so much with myself about what to do, but I knew that ultimately, I could not miss their special day.

With Lee's help, I decided to rewrite the script about what January 25th meant. I was never going to forget that day, but the universe had given me an opportunity to change how I viewed it. It no longer had to be about pain, fear, trauma and devastation. They had already happened and I could never change that, but I did not need to keep living through the event as I did each year on the anniversary. This was an opportunity to remember this day as a celebration of love, with friends who I cherish.

Getting my head around this was a lot more difficult than it sounds. I had to do a lot of planning on how I would get there, how I would manage if things became too much and what I would do if I needed to leave. Lee helped me work through all of this and we made a safety plan for how I would get through the day. This really helped me to see that it was nothing about the date, the day, who I was with. Those two men were not going to turn up at the wedding because I had chosen to celebrate that day. They were not going to be there on my way home just because it was the 25th of January. So many of these thoughts had been distorted in my head without me realising, and this challenge gave me the opportunity to work through it, processing more of the pieces of the jigsaw.

So on the 25th of January 2020, I woke up feeling OK – anxious but not overwhelmingly so. I got a message from Lee which read:

> *'I feel like today is the first day of the rest of my life. I will say goodbye to anything that is not in my best interest and I will only allow good things into my life going forward. I must say goodbye to anyone that has hurt me and I will offer a great big smile and welcome all the opportunities placed before me. I deserve so much better in life, good things are coming my way, and I am better and better every day. Thank you God for pushing me to grow into who I am today. I believe the best is yet to come. '*

I really felt every word of that message and for the first time ever I remember telling myself, 'yeah, you do deserve better.' I seemed to get an inner strength from somewhere, a spark and a sense of fight that I wasn't used to, and I actually felt quite excited to get my hair and makeup done.

Watching Kirsty and Gary take their vows was the best part of the day for me and it was what will hopefully change my memories of that terrible date. It sounds like a cliché, but the love that exuded from Kirsty and Gary and the involvement of their family just filled my heart with happiness. I cried the whole way through the service. I cried at how beautiful Kirsty looked, at her daughters Ella and Eva reading their poems, at Ella crying with happiness for her mum and dad, at the way Gary looked at Kirsty. All of it was so emotional, but for happy reasons.

My thoughts did wander at times during the ceremony. If this date was different for me, then maybe I would have been able to stand in a beautiful dress with someone looking at me like that. I had dreamed of getting married since I was a little girl. I remember designing what my wedding dress would look like and fantasising about where my wedding would take place. I could not imagine what it would be like for someone to have that much love for you and want to be with you for the rest of their life. That dream had been stolen from me, like so many others. I was working hard to unhook and bring my thoughts back to why I was there that day – for Kirsty and Gary.

I did have several wobbles through the day, but not on the scale I was expecting. I could feel panic building from my stomach at certain times, especially when we went into the evening reception. People were getting more and more intoxicated and I could feel my head starting to spin. I felt like I was being triggered by something, but I did not know what.

I was not aware of this at the time, but I have since learned that my body's way of coping with extreme stress and panic was to shut off – sometimes making me faint. This is the route I felt I was going down, but I had the plan in place that Lee and I had made and I knew I had to just take a step away for a while to calm my thoughts. I was able to get out to my car and text Lee, who then helped me with some breathing.

I had set myself a challenge to focus on each hour at a time and then review how I was feeling. I was hoping to push myself to get to as near close to midnight as I could. I wanted to prove to my subconscious that nothing bad was going to happen on this night and at that time. There was actually an hour or two when I didn't check my watch as I was just in the present moment, enjoying the time with some of the evening guests.

I had made it to 10.30 when the girls I was with decided they were ready to go home. I was the designated driver and was happy with what I had achieved, so we said our goodbyes and left. The journey home took longer than expected as there were road closures and we had to do a few detours. As I dropped the girls off, I realised that it was going to be about 1145pm when I got home – the time I had dreaded all day. When I realised this, I felt sick and panic was building. I thought about going for a further drive, just so I could forget about the time 16 years before that had changed my life forever. I was able to rationalise my thoughts and thanks to the work I had done with Lee, I was able to remind myself that these were in fact just thoughts.

CHAPTER 16

# The Pandemic

*'What's the best thing you've learned about storms? That they end, said the horse.' – Charlie Mackesey, The Boy, the Mole, the Fox and the Horse*

Towards the end of January, the media had begun reporting news about a virus that had swept across China and threatened to spread across the world. Little did we know then what a devastating effect Covid 19 would have on everybody's lives and how it would literally make the world stop. I hadn't been overly worried about it. I chose to stop watching the news when Lucy was born in a bid to try to live more in the moment. Some might say it was ignorance or naivety, but I wasn't overly concerned. I was focusing on the intentions I had set and my determination to make 2020 a better year.

I saw on Facebook that Madeleine Black was going to be speaking at an event at the Blythswood Hotel. I had mentioned it to Lee and said I would love to hear her speaking in person as I had been so blown away by her Ted Talk and her book. Lee said, well let's do it then, let's go! I automatically shut it down and said I couldn't as it was in the middle of Glasgow – a place I just did not go. Lee planted the seed that this year I wanted to try and face my fears – and what better way than to go and see someone who was inspirational to me and also give to charity as it was a charity dinner. Lee left the thought with me, not pushing or forcing me, but enough to make me think, maybe I could do this. She was good at that – planting the seed and letting me work it out and get there on my own.

I booked the tickets, along with an overnight stay for us both. Part of the reason for this was that the thought of getting home from town was too much to handle as Lee and I lived in opposite directions. Staying overnight in Glasgow was also terrifying. so either way, I knew I was going to be pushed way out of my comfort zone. My focus for the next month was on how I was going to be able to deal with this.

There was news flying in about the Coronavirus spreading like wildfire and the outbreak had now been officially classed as a pandemic, as it was sweeping across the world. Devastating figures for death rates were coming in from China and Italy and there were now reported cases in Britain. A lot of people around me were starting to panic about what this meant for us. I had not quite caught up with that anxiety yet (which was unusual), as I was still focused on how I was going to get through a night at the Blythswood in the middle of Glasgow. It really showed how much trauma had distorted my view of reality, as I was still focusing on a threat from almost 20 years ago. Now there was a real live threat heading towards us and I was not letting it bother me – yet!

Towards the start of March, everybody's anxiety levels were heightened. People were starting to panic-buy food (and toilet rolls!), holidays were being cancelled and there was talk of shutting down the country. It was at this point I started to panic, as there was an echo of dread creeping into my psyche. It wasn't actually about catching the virus, more about what I would do without my support network. I had been seeing someone weekly for my mental health since the end of 2017, and I could not comprehend how I would manage without it. I tried to put it aside and pray that it was all scaremongering so I could focus on my upcoming event at the Blythswood. Lee and I had worked on a safety plan to get there and what I would do to remain in control if I started to feel triggered or panicked.

March 6th 2020 was the Say Women event at the Blythswood Square Hotel. I made it there safely! Lee and I got there early and checked into our room. I had parked my car in an overnight car park a few streets away. In my head, the walk from the car to the hotel felt like walking through a war zone. I think I held my breath the whole five minutes it took us to get there. This was a hauntingly familiar strategy, the one that had got me through that night. I could hear sounds in my head, I was aware of passing alleyways similar to the one I had been dragged down, and I was waiting for those two men to jump out from one of them and say 'we told you never to tell anyone!' But I made it, despite a great effort from my unresolved trauma and negative chatter to try and stop me.

During the evening, safety precautions had been introduced as a mitigation for Covid 19. People were advised not to shake hands, not to hug and to wash their hands regularly. Lee and I went into the bar before the meal. I remember seeing Madeleine in the corner and feeling so starstruck. I was in awe of this woman; her strength, her motivation, everything about her just radiated inspiration. She was also very beautiful. I looked at her and thought, if you can overcome everything that you went through, then hopefully I can too.

During Madeleine's talk, I was moved to tears – again! The way she told her story, the passion behind her work to support people and the determination she had to heal inspired me on a different level. Difficult as that night was to overcome, I made it, and I felt a small sense of achievement that I had faced fear right in the eye and pushed right through it.

In the next few weeks, panic levels for the whole country rose to a level I had never experienced. I was used to feeling like this, but now everyone around me was falling apart too. The country was about to plunge into lockdown. Preparations were being made for schools and nurseries to close, and people were being told to isolate and stay at home if they were vulnerable. The three main symptoms – a dry cough, a temperature and shortness of breath – were highlighted, and this led people to panic if they started to feel the least bit unwell.

I remember trying to make final arrangements for our nursery to close. We were moving into the local primary school as part of a community hub to support keyworker children and children in need. Trudy was already isolating as she had a cough, so I was in charge of communicating with parents, trying to reassure staff, moving furniture from one building into another, and it was crazy times. I too had started to feel unwell with a pounding headache and a sore throat, but this wasn't any of the identified symptoms, so I believed the headache to be down to stress.

Nobody was allowed to visit anyone's house, and you could only meet in small groups outdoors. On the 16th of March, which was also Mother's Day, my family decided to have one last family walk around a local football playing field. We were all socially distanced, walking around at what can only be described as a surreal time. We said goodbye not knowing when we would see each other again or what was going to happen. We were told that there would be a national lockdown for three weeks to try and get the numbers of people contracting Covid 19 under control. We were all scared, as nobody knew what was coming next or when we would see each other again. I had just been blessed with the most beautiful little nephew four weeks earlier and could not believe that I didn't know when I would be able to hold him again.

On the 17th of March 2020, I started to believe that I might have Covid. I had a headache that I could not describe and I felt so exhausted that I could hardly get out of bed. I spent the next three days in bed with the worst headache I had ever experienced, and nothing would take it away. By day 4 I was unable to get up and go downstairs. I told my mum and dad to avoid me in case it was Covid, but I could not do the same with Lucy. I wanted to try and reassure her that everything was going to be ok, as the world as we knew it seemed to be falling apart.

During the next few days, my chest started to feel quite tight, but the headache had lifted slightly, so it was manageable. There were no tests available at this time – only people who were admitted to hospital were given tests – so I still wasn't sure if it was Covid or not.

Day 9 came, and that was when things got serious. I had felt a bit breathless the last few days, but thought it was down to my own panicking. However, on day 9, I really couldn't get a breath. My chest felt like someone had put a firework inside it, and the burning pain was unbearable. I tried to persevere as long as I could as I knew the NHS was already overwhelmed with people contacting them with symptoms, so I was trying to breathe through it, but I literally couldn't.

I phoned 111 and was sent to a Covid Assessment Centre on the other side of Glasgow. I had to drive myself there as I couldn't risk my mum or dad being in the car with me. Lucy was asleep and thankfully unaware of how bad I had got.

The 30-minute drive to the hospital was terrible. I felt like I was gasping for air and was convinced that if I didn't die of Covid, I was going to crash the car on the way to hospital. All sorts of things were going through my head. For someone who did not normally watch the news, I had become glued to it, looking for someone to tell us the way out of this situation. I had seen people in hospital and heard stories of healthy people being wiped out by the virus – was I going to be one of these statistics?

I drove over the Kingston Bridge with tears streaming down my face, thinking I had never even said cheerio to Lucy. What if she woke up in the morning and I was gone? What if I never got to see my mum and dad again? Nobody really knew how unwell I was. What if they just heard on the news that I was one of those people who had been struck by the virus and died? I knew I was getting very irrational, but I had no one with me to reassure me, so my mind was running away with me. It also triggered some very painful memories of what I had felt 'that night' – that I was going to die.

I was checked over by the hospital by a doctor, who said that my oxygen levels weren't low enough to be admitted to hospital and that basically, I just had to ride it out. They couldn't offer me a test as there weren't any available yet, and they tried to play down the fact that it could be Covid by saying there were lots of viruses going around. The nurse who was taking my vitals said that it was more than likely Covid, but I was better off at home.

I could never have imagined what was to come in the next few months. I once again lost the person I was. I went from being a young, fit, healthy 38-year-old to feeling like someone who could hardly walk, struggled to breathe, had zero energy and was plagued with fatigue. I spent weeks in my bed and was left exhausted by simply walking to the toilet. I was sent back to the hospital several times for more tests, chest X-rays, heart scans and

CT scans, but they could find nothing. I could not be diagnosed with what they were classing as long Covid because I had never received a positive test – no one had at that time. I started to feel that nobody believed I was really feeling these things as I hadn't had that test result and nothing was showing up on any scans. When I phoned up again with constant breathlessness, my GP would ask, 'do you think you are just panicking?' Of course I was panicking, who wouldn't when they felt they could not breathe, but I was very well versed in panic attacks and could easily identify the difference. I felt like I was begging someone to help me, but nobody was listening. Again, not being believed and not being listened too were very familiar worries. Now, looking back, I know that this was because nobody really knew what to do. Health professionals were learning as they went along with this new virus and were already at breaking point in trying to manage the fallout from it.

The isolation I felt during this time was unbearable. Everybody had retreated into their own worlds as a survival mechanism to cope with the never-ending lockdown, which was understandable. It was just me, my mum and dad and Lucy and four walls. I couldn't even take Lucy out on the 1 hour outdoor exercise time that we were allowed to have as I wasn't fit enough. I don't know what I would have done without my mum and dad, as they had to take over the reins in taking care of her for me.

One of the hardest parts of having Covid was having my little girl ask me, 'Who is going to look after me when you die?' I had tried to shield her from the news and what was going on in the world, but she was smart, she could sense the fear in my home that I was not ok, she could hear telephone calls, and she would walk in when the news was on. My heart actually broke when she asked me this and I reassured her that I was not going anywhere, even though I was not sure of that myself.

Fast forward 14 months and I had been in and out of work, living one of the most horrendous years I could remember. I received my first vaccine at this time, and it felt like a miracle cure. My symptoms started to get less intense, I had more energy, and I could push myself to do more physical exertion and didn't end up in bed for a week after trying to recover. I was finally seeing some light at the end of a very dark tunnel.

Contracting Covid taught me many things. For one thing, it made me stop, literally. Even though I had engaged in counselling for the last three years, I still had not managed to stop and sit still with anything. I would try and work through things, then put a face on and get back to my day-to-day life, all the while dying inside. Covid took that choice away from me. I was stuck in my bed, stuck within the four walls of my home and being told by the Government I was not allowed to go anywhere.

Of course during this time, a lot of things came up that I could no longer run away from. In my journey with Lee, I had started to face what happened to me, but now was the time (an opportunity) to start dealing with it. It was also quite ironic that the place I believe I had contracted the virus was in fact the charity event at the Blythswood. The place where I had overcome many fears was the place that was to take my healing journey to a different level.

CHAPTER 17

# Going in...

*'Healing occurs when we bring up the courage to stay present with our deep 'raw pain', even if it's just for a few moments.'* – Tanja Windegger

Not being able to run from myself was the hardest yet most critical thing I had to do. My sessions with Lee had now become virtual, like most of the world. Face-to-face communication had disappeared and everything had to be done through a telephone or on screen. I missed the contact we had during these sessions, I missed hugs, and I missed being held physically as well as emotionally. I was so grateful that Lee was able to continue with our sessions, because I don't know how I would have survived lockdown without her.

We began working on and sitting with difficult memories and emotions. This had been something that I had avoided and I had allowed myself to create a whole new, distorted reality in my head.

I had been left with many fears and phobias after my attack, so we started to sit and unpick them. One of these had been a fear of taxis. I hadn't had much recollection of the actual taxi journey itself, yet I was left with an indescribable and irrational fear of taxis. My memories were only brought back to life when I explored this with Lee. We explored what role the taxi had played in my story of that night. When sitting with the memory, I was able to answer Lee's questions, questions I had never asked or answered myself. What did I remember from inside the taxi? Did I speak to the taxi driver? What route did I take home? Did I have a phone? How did I pay? Through sitting with these memories, I was able to plough through some of the details, and that helped me work out things in my head which then helped me to address and change unhelpful thought patterns.

As I had sat inside the taxi on the way home, I remember how soft and padded the seat was. It was a seat that went all across the back, like a big padded cushion across the whole seat. I sat nearest the door so that I didn't have to move too far to get in and out. My motivation for getting through that taxi journey was 'don't let the taxi driver see the blood'. I had tissue inserted inside to try and stop the blood, but that soon became soaked through. I remember constantly dabbling the blood with my skirt to ensure that none of it went on his seat. I knew before I even got in the taxi that I could not say anything to the taxi driver in case he took me to the police station. If that happened, what the two men had said to me would come true. They would find me and they would kill me.

It's amazing what your memory holds even when you have

never thought about it, something I discovered throughout this process, both in my body and in my mind. I had no clue where my jacket went that night, and when Lee asked about how I paid for the taxi, I could not remember, I didn't even know if I had a bag. But gradually as we worked through story, I remembered that I had had a bag as that was where I got the tissues from. But as for my purse and my phone, I don't remember using them at any point and don't have any memory of where they ended up.

Working through this memory allowed me to see that the taxi journey was actually my route to safety that night. It was the taxi that took me away from danger and back to the safety of my house. Up until now, my memories had been about the compounding fear I had when in the taxi, but in reality that was nothing to do with the taxi journey itself.

Neither the taxi nor the taxi driver were the threat that night, they were my route to safety, and had I not got into that taxi, I might not be here now writing this. I also worked out that I didn't actually have a fear of taxis, I had a fear of getting to a taxi on my own. That was my plan that night, leave the club and go get a taxi. I didn't need to phone one as I knew the taxi rank was at the bottom of the street. Unfortunately, I never got there.

CHAPTER 18

# Acknowledging the grief

*'A piece of my heart has wings'*

Another memory that we chose to sit with was one that took me completely by surprise as to how much emotion I had wrapped around it. I had lost a baby and never allowed myself to feel anything about that loss. I had wrapped it up in a mixture of guilt and shame and buried it so deep that I never gave myself permission to deal with it.

I remember that when I decided to have Lucy, the emotional turmoil I had buried so deeply about the miscarriage came flooding back. I could not talk to anyone about it as I felt so ashamed of what I had done and was worried that 'they' would not let me have another chance. I managed to bury these emotions and thoughts at that time and my desperation to have another chance at becoming a mum won over everything else.

These feelings and irrational thoughts came back in waves many times during the IVF, pregnancy and birth. I told myself that I didn't deserve this to happen. I questioned whether I was going to be punished in some way. I believed that Lucy would be taken away from me, just as I had taken away my other baby's life. Again, I used that old coping strategy of disconnecting to get me through.

When I finally spoke to Lee about the miscarriage, I had no idea how much it had affected me. I had spoken to her about 'feeling a presence' in the last few weeks that I had associated with dark feelings and the men that attacked me. Lee suggested to me, could it be the presence of this little baby? I felt an overwhelming feeling of grief, a grief that I had never allowed myself to feel because I had conditioned my brain into thinking I didn't have the right to grieve something I had caused. Lee suggested that maybe this presence was the baby being around to tell me to finally let go!

I had not told Lee that I had been finding that week particularly hard. My close friend had miscarried her baby the previous year and it would have been due to be born now. My heart felt heavy for her sadness, as I knew how much she had longed for that baby. She had done nothing wrong to miscarry and she was totally broken by it.

Lee explored with me the fact that I had done nothing wrong either. She asked if I would have been able to cope with a baby at that time. I had explored this a few years earlier with Karen during a therapy session. I absolutely believed that I would not have coped with a baby in my physical or mental state, but I was still entrenched in guilt. We also spoke about the likelihood of the overdose causing the miscarriage. The chances are that the miscarriage would have happened anyway as a result of the cortisol levels I would have been producing at that time and the trauma I had been through. Way back then, could this have been 'the universe having my back'?

Lee asked me how I would feel about resolving to finally let the guilt go and see that 'presence' as a positive – a little person looking out for me. I could not feel anything other than overwhelming sadness. I know that if it was meant to be and I had carried the baby to term, I would have loved it with every piece of my heart, but would I want a wee baby to born in such horrific circumstances? Not really!

After a few sessions, something happened. I started to feel a new lightness inside and I finally felt I had let go of something. I decided to put my trust in the universe, believing that it had other plans for that wee baby, and for me. If it had worked out differently, I would not have had Lucy – someone I could not live without!

I am beyond grateful that I have been given the gift of being a mum and will always see that as the greatest achievement of my life.

CHAPTER 19

# Dear younger self...

*'Dear past me. Holy shit you can fight a fight. Thank you for never giving up even though you've wanted to countless times. You've taught me that there is nothing I cant get through. I owe my relentless strength to you.'* – Rita Jade

I had managed to work through so much with Lee during lockdown. It was a hard slog and extremely exhausting. I was struggling with the lack of physical contact and support, something you couldn't get from online contact.

In July 2020, as the world was gradually opening up, Lee and I were allowed to meet for socially distanced walks. Social distancing was the biggest buzz word that came out of 2020! We would meet and walk around parks and enjoy being back in nature. This was something that many people really found comfort in during lockdown, as it was one of the few things we were allowed to do.

On one of our walks, Lee said that she wanted to try and help me reconnect with my younger self in a bid to 'let it go'. I said that I would never be able to do this out in nature. No venues were opened back up yet after lockdown, so it was difficult to decide where would be the best place to do it. We talked about having a girly overnight in a local hotel, where we could work on the hard stuff first, then enjoy some girlie time.

Something special happened that weekend, something that I never thought possible. I was able to write this letter to myself:

> *Friday the 28th of August was the first day in nearly 18 years when I connected back with someone who I hated with every part of my being. I was disgusted by that person, was so ashamed of that person and never wanted her to enter my thoughts and would push them away with everything I had. The person that I'm referring to is you (me), an innocent 21-year-old girl who was robbed of everything she ever knew in the space of a few hours.*
>
> *I've left you in a place that neither of us wanted to be and blamed you for something that could never have been your fault. You've been trapped and left paralysed in a scene that I can only describe as torturous. Whilst I've been physically able to move away from it, I've left you stuck there reliving & replaying the most abhorrent scenes, scenes anyone would struggle to imagine.*
>
> *Today I'm not going to let you stay there any longer. I left a big part of my heart and soul there with*

*u that night, and now it needs to come back where it belongs .....as one ♥.*

*I know I'll never be the person I was when I left you there, but the person that's coming back to get you isn't as bad as she's been left to believe she is. Hopefully we can come back together – stronger than ever.*

*Friday was a special day in my journey of healing. Lee has spoken in the last year of going back to get 21-year-old me and bringing her home. Every time she has said it, it felt right in my heart. It's something that I've been desperate but terrified to do, yet I've had no clue how we would do it. After a lot of revisiting, Lee gave me my first Reiki session in the hotel room. Once it was finished, she told me to give her a hug and welcome 'you' back.*

*When she said we were going to do that, I was sceptical and thought, well I'll give Lee a hug and that will make me feel better, but I can't hug someone that's not here. When I did hug her, I felt something I didn't expect. I felt an overwhelming sadness and sorrow for 'that person' that I've hated for the last 17 years. I held her so tight, like the way I wish someone had held me after that night. Tight enough to hold their pain, let them know they were not alone and that everything would be OK. I wanted to say sorry for the way I've treated her, how could I be so cruel? I would never treat anyone that way, never mind someone that had been through something so horrific.*

*I wanted to say sorry to... you, to me, to us, because we are that one person. I could not have survived that night without you!! And you can't get back here without me, so now it's time to come together as one again.*

*I made it here today because of the strength and fight you had that night. For many years I've blamed you for not giving up and making me face what happened when it would have been easier if you just gave up and died. I've wished that I could hand my brain over to someone else and have them erase the imprint of the trauma that was so deeply buried. Having experienced that feeling again on some level this weekend, I am in awe of how you faced death right in the eye and held on to life so tight.*

*This was not your fault, it was forced upon you, and you did not give up on that fight which was so unfair, so I'm not going to give up and leave u there now. We need to come together again and make sure the best revenge is letting go and moving on. (This may take a while, so you might need to give me some time.)*

*I've had a photo of you (me) hidden away for so, so long. A photo of all of us in the limo the night of Karen's birthday. That was the last picture I had of me happy, smiling, carefree and invincible.*

*Looking at this picture would was beyond painful and something that terrified me to do. I did not want to see you, as your clothes reminded me of the broken body underneath that they hid. The smile on your face reminded me of a smile I could never have again, your face reminded me of any carefreeness and innocence that was to be stolen.*

*I hated the person, I hated you! 21-year-old you reminded me of the worst experience of my life and I blamed you for every part of that night. But something has finally clicked. I do not hate you, I hate what happened to you – to us. And it was easier to hate you than face the magnitude of that night. This is something that has been said to me over and over again, but I cannot tell you the difference between hearing it and the power of feeling it.*

*When I look at that photo now, I don't look at it in disgust and hatred, I look at it with the greatest sadness, knowing what you (we) were about to go through. Something that was completely out of our control and that would have such devastating consequences for how the next part of our life would unfold. We did not ask for any of this, we were entitled to have a night out with friends, making the choices we did and still get home safe. Everything we did that night was a testament to our bravery and courage and undeniable strength*

*So I'm going to love you the way you should have been after that night. I'm not leaving us behind any more to be stuck in a world of pain and suffering – that no longer exists. I need your strength to get us both through this next chapter of healing and I'll let you into the amazing parts of my world that I have been lucky enough to find.*

*Let's Retake ALL Power & Exhale (RAPE) and see the 'us' as a survivor of rape and warrior that we are. We can take our power back together and hopefully use it to help others on the same journey one day.*

CHAPTER 20

# Coping strategies

*'Before you pass judgement on one who is self-destructing, it's important to remember they usually aren't trying to destroy themselves. They're trying to destroy something inside that doesn't belong.' – JM Storm*

Another of my sessions with Lee that really stands out was when I finally addressed coping strategies. My journey with self-harm has been a very confusing one for me to get my head round and even harder to try and explain to other people. Those without any experience of trauma may find this difficult to understand, but I have been lucky that the few people I have confided in have wrapped me up in kindness and understanding and helped me work my way through it.

The first time I tried self-harming as a coping mechanism it was actually (in my head) an attempt to end my life. I was feeling so low and trapped in my thoughts that I looked at the veins on my wrist and pulled a razor blade across them. My subconscious, the universe, whatever you want to call it, was probably guiding me way back then, as I clearly did not cut deep or long enough to rupture any veins. In the moment, I was terrified by the amount of blood pouring out, felt dizzy and became consumed with trying to get it to stop. In that moment I was exactly that – in that moment. I had managed to get out of my head, stop my thoughts and focus on a different kind of pain.

This was where my relationship with self-harm began. On days when I was struggling with thoughts and memories, it would be my coping strategy to get them away. The memories I had back then were very limited, or what I would let in was very limited. I had no memory of pain in my body at this point, it was purely in my head, and any time it entered my thoughts and I couldn't get it away, I would resort to self-harming to take the mental torture away. By doing this, it gave me a physical pain that I knew was real. The mental pain felt so excruciating inside that I always felt that if I had a 'real' pain from harming myself, it would be more justified.

I also felt I deserved to feel the physical pain, I had deserved what had happened to my body that night, and I deserved to continue to suffer as a result of what I had done. I do know now that this is not the case, but for me, cutting would bring me back to what was going on in the present and reaffirm that I deserved to be punished in some way.

The first few times I did it, I was not clever enough to keep it hidden. I cut my wrists, my thigh, my arm, my leg and would make excuses that I had had a fall or an injury of some sort if anyone noticed it. As the years went on, I became more aware of cutting in places that could not be seen.

I have not used cutting as a coping strategy for the last 18 years. I have used it on and off and have gone years in between using it. This really reflects my journey with my trauma, as there have been long periods of time when the memories have been pushed so deep that they have not been an issue for me.

I would say that in the last few years, I have had a real internal struggle with self-harm. As I entered deeper into my healing journey with Karen and Lee, my story materialised more than I could ever have known it would, and I could never have imagined what the impact would be, physically and mentally.

As the memories became more painful, my need to take myself out of my head became greater. And then memories of the physical pain to my body came to remind me in another way. The pain I started feeling in my vagina and abdominal area was something I could not handle, and I felt like I was going to go insane. I would try and keep the memories and my thoughts separate to what the physical pain was because I was terrified if the 2 would collide, then I would die!! I know that sounds very dramatic, but this feeling was very much alive in my body and mind.

I began cutting in the area that had been hurt the most, an area that no one would ever be able to see and an area that I felt deserved to be in pain and to be tortured, just as it had been that night. This would sound ludicrous to anyone listening, which is why I have only ever told one person, someone who has never judged me or made me feel bad about the strategies I had to use to help me to cope. She would make me feel safe to tell her, ask if I was physically OK and offer to support me get help medically if I needed it, whilst always trying to reassure me that this was a way of coping with something so traumatic. With the help of Lee, I was able to work through my self-harming journey and completely change my own mind-set about it. I would use these strategies to numb thoughts and pain, but Lee helped me see that the few minutes of short-term gain I got from doing this were having a detrimental impact on my self-esteem and self-worth, as well as my being impacted physically – again.

During lockdown, I became terrified on two occasions that I might have done myself serious harm and the consequences of this would definitely outweigh the benefits. Lee had asked me in the past if hurting myself in this place would not trigger more hurtful thoughts and memories of what happened that night. I would say, up until now, it had actually not. Doing this never seemed to trigger the pain of that night, partly because I had never allowed myself these memories a chance to resurface.

Being stabbed in that area is something that I had never really known about, or when I did know, I could not allow myself to accept the magnitude of it. I would never allow my mind to process the impact or engage with the physical feelings.

Working with Lee through this part of my trauma allowed me to see the magnitude of that part of my attack and to put these two pieces of the puzzle together. I then began to see that cutting in this area is actually more of a trigger than a support. It began to take me closer to my trauma instead of further away from it, as I longed to be.

I would never judge anyone who has used or who uses self-harming as a way of coping, but speaking from the other side of it, I can now say that it is something that can be worked through with the right support.

CHAPTER 21

# Body image

*'You don't have to learn how to love yourself, you just have to remember there was nothing wrong with you to begin with. You just have to come home.' – Nayyirah Waheed*

My body image was completely shattered after that night. As many victims of rape and sexual assault know, your body no longer feels your own. You feel disgusted, repulsed and disconnected from something that once felt like it belonged to you. No amount of cleaning can take the feeling of dirt and contamination away.

It took me a long time to acknowledge that another of my coping strategies had in fact been developing an eating disorder. I didn't start out with that intention, but I suppose nobody does. I initially had no appetite or inclination to eat. I felt physically sick all the time, so didn't want to put food into my body to risk vomiting. I was terrified of being sick as a child. I would feel like I was choking and couldn't breathe, so it was never my intention to ultimately start making myself sick and adding to this fear.

My body image had already become very distorted by what had happened. I dropped from a size 16 to a size 10/12 in a matter of months. I had no awareness of looking any different, as all I could feel was a sense of loathing at the body I had that felt so broken.

I didn't start to make myself sick for a few years after, and I don't really remember what made me do it for the first time. I think it was a combination of feeling repulsed by my body, and it was also something that took my head away from the thoughts and memories I was desperately trying to push away. Those few minutes of being sick gave my head some peace from the feelings of insanity that swirled around my brain.

I had convinced my mind that if I started to gain weight and go back to the same weight I was when it happened, then it was going to happen again. I developed this irrational fear that I couldn't go past a certain number on the scale or I was asking to raped all over again. The thought of even thinking those words, 'asking' to be raped, makes my skin crawl now. I can't believe that I let people do this to my mind and make it justifiable to myself that women would ask to be raped. Of course I know now that the only cause of rape is the men who chose to do it, it has nothing to do with the victim.

I began to tell myself that being sick would be a way of finally getting rid of everything that was in my body, especially in my mouth. This was all part of the mental torture that I was going through because of the actions of those two men. Unfortunately, I had turned the blame inward. Each time I would feel a sense of relief that it was gone but unfortunately these feelings did not last. Being sick was never going to take that feeling away, because the feelings and thoughts were trapped somewhere in my head that I wasn't ready to address.

I never told anyone about my eating disorder, although I'm sure many people guessed as my weight would plummet at times of severe stress and anxiety. My means of coping this way were very much determined by my thoughts and feelings. I could not always articulate what they were, it's only now that I understand this was my mind trying to get my attention. I was trying so hard to hide everything from the outside world and thought I was doing a good job of it, pretending it had never happened, but my trauma was seeping through and taking its toll on my body.

My fear of being sick as a child has never really gone away, yet I continued to do it. I guess this was another way of me subconsciously punishing my body. It never entered my head that looking after the body that felt so broken and damaged might actually be the way out of this.

I manage to control this when I decided to go ahead with my treatment to have Lucy. I knew that I would have to nourish my body in some way in order to carry a child. I did struggle with putting on weight when I was pregnant, but I would never let myself do anything that could damage or harm my baby. My body was no longer about what happened during that time. It had a purpose, and that purpose was making sure I was growing a healthy little baby.

During the first few years of Lucy's life, I felt no need to go back to old coping strategies. I wouldn't say I was happy with my body, I was just so consumed with my time with Lucy and my love for her that I didn't allow any thoughts to come. I think that disassociation played a part again in allowing me to enjoy this time with the gift I had longed for, but as with any trauma, if it's unresolved, it will always find a way to get your attention.

I have continued to struggle with my weight on and off in the last four years and it does usually become an issue when I have been triggered again. I have photos that I look back on now remember how disgusting and overweight I felt at the time they were taken. I also remember how I was feeling at that time and know that I was not in a good place. These photos let me see how thin I actually was. It's only been recently that I have begun to see that was never about me being fat or disgusting or repulsive. This was my trauma controlling my thoughts and behaviours. I feel that metaphorically I may have felt so heavy as I was carrying so much trauma in my head, in my body and in my cells; it was nothing to do with my physical weight. In the last year that feeling has really shifted for me and I feel so much lighter mentally. My weight goes up and down like that of any woman, and a pandemic certainly doesn't help the waistline, but I no longer feel that inner heaviness that I used to feel.

CHAPTER 22

# Rewriting the script

*'What if I fall? Oh, but my darling, what if you fly?'*
*– Eric Harrison*

As 2020 came to an end, I was so glad to see the end of another horrendous year. Covid had shut the world down and changed the way we lived. However, I had actually achieved a lot in 2020 in terms of healing from trauma. At the time, I thought that Covid had wasted the year when I wanted to change everything, when I wanted to start a new decade and leave the past where it belonged. In actual fact, it gave me the time to face many demons and to start to face something I had never addressed before – myself!

We went into another lockdown in December 2020, which lasted for a further three months. During this time when everyone was fed up with the world, I was able to face one of my biggest fears, marking a weekend that usually had me in a dark place. I took control and tried to change the script of a story that no longer served me.

On 24th of January 2021, I met Lee for a socially distanced walk after she had been for her vaccination at the Louisa Jordan. We walked along the Clyde side for a bit before sitting on a bench for a chat. I found it very difficult not to break down in front of her as we were in a public place. It had been a really difficult time for everyone going back into lockdown and I couldn't bear going back to virtual sessions after we had got back to meeting face to face again.

After talking for a while, Lee asked if I wanted to head towards town and see how far we could go. She said that she didn't want me to get to the point where fear took over my body, so I had to tell her when it got too much, that I was in control and we could turn back at any point.

I had an overwhelming sense of, 'Yes let's do this!'! It was a beautiful day, I loved walking near the water, it was about as quiet as the town was ever going to be – and Lee was right beside me. I said, let's go for it. As we were walking along, I knew Lee was talking a lot of nonsense to keep my mind in the present moment. It did actually work – to a point. As we walked along, she would check in with me and see where I was on a scale of 1-10. I surprised myself at being at a 3!

As we got closer to turn down towards Argyle Street, I could feel my legs starting to shake. I tried to walk a bit quicker so I didn't notice. I could hear Lee talking and reassuring me, although I felt like my head was somewhere different, not in the place where I thought it would have gone. I felt so determined to keep going, and I was thinking about New York, and all the places I love to walk, I was thinking about 'feeling the fear and doing it anyway' and I thought, I haven't come this far, to only come this far!

Lee talked me through all the places we were going and where we could stop to have a cup of tea to decide if I wanted to go a bit further. I knew if I stopped, my head would take over, so I decided to let the adrenaline take me. I just had to keep going or I wouldn't go at all.

When I saw Buchanan Street, I knew how close we were. Lee told me that we were just about to see the Debenhams sign, the sign that should remind me of the survivor I had been that night, where I should face what I had gone through and walk towards that sign – that showed my strength.

We stopped underneath it and Lee told me to take a picture. In my head I was thinking, how am I here? I always said I could never come back here.

Lee asked if I wanted to cross the road to the Next store and take the picture from the direction I would have seen it, walking towards it. Again, I just wanted to keep going. I was so curious and terrified at the same time to see what was at the bottom of that lane. We stopped at the corner and I took a picture from that direction, of the way I had seen the sign that night. I could feel my emotions starting to reach the surface. I remembered so vividly seeing that sign after what I had just endured. I remembered feeling numb but broken, lost and disorientated, but determined to be normal and go home. The sign that haunted for me for years was actually the sign that I was reaching safety.

I could feel my heart pounding out my chest and I felt sick with fear, but I knew I wasn't done. I asked Lee if I could walk up just a little further to the lane, to see what was there – if anyone was there. At this point I didn't think I was going to make it. My feet were walking forward, but I was scared to turn round and look. Although this was crazy, I was scared I was going to see those two men at the end of the lane – whether they were just in my head or would be there in person. All rational thoughts of the possibility of this not being possible were starting to leave me.

My adrenaline was moving my feet now. I had a quick look down and saw the lane, which had a gate at the end now, and I could see there was no one there. They weren't there any more, but more importantly, neither was I! The image I had in my head was gone and replaced with a new one.

That overwhelming sense of grit and determination I had to get me there, was now replaced with an overwhelming sense of 'I need to get out of here, now!!' I could feel the tears starting to stream down my face, I felt dizzy and I thought I couldn't breathe.

Lee scooped my arm up and we started walking. I could hear her telling me how proud she was of me and that I was safe, but in my head I was just trying not to faint.

As we got further away, I had a horrible feeling that someone was behind me. Lee made me challenge this thought and turn round to see that I was safe and there was nothing around me that posed any risk. We then practised some breathing and I could feel myself coming back into my body.

I could feel the noisy chatter in my head taking over and thinking, what if I've done the wrong thing by doing this? What if seeing this place would make my memories more real? Again Lee made me challenge this – I had done nothing wrong and every time I felt my head going there I was to look at that photo as a sign of how brave I was and the survivor I was, both then and now.

As we walked back along the Clyde side, I could feel myself starting to get infected by Lee's buzzing exhilaration that I had managed to achieve that. I couldn't believe I had done that. I had never, ever thought I would be able to go back to that place and face that fear dead in the eye.

I think I went through every emotion on that walk back – fear, terror, shock, sadness, surprise – and even a wee bit of pride in myself. The universe was definitely trying to get me to come to terms with my trauma. Every year up until then, I had mourned this date as the anniversary as the most terrible day of my life. I had done everything to avoid anything to do with Burns day. I would always keep myself busy, but this year, I had nowhere to go and no one to be with other than myself, and that day reminded me of the fighter I was that night and how my determination had got me through all the years so far.

This was the start of me re-writing the script and being responsible for the next chapters in my life. With my 40th birthday coming up in October, I was starting to believe that 'life could begin at 40'.

CHAPTER 23

# The see me, hear me blog

*'Our job is not to deny the story, but to defy the ending – to rise strong, recognize our story, and rumble with the truth until we get to a place where we think, Yes, this is what happened and I will choose how the story ends.'* – Brene Brown

Having faced one of my biggest fears by going back to the place where I was raped, I had found a new drive that pushed me into doing my next challenge. I had followed the training company Epione on social media and had attended one of their events in 2019. I was deeply impressed by their passion to support victims of trauma and their drive to work towards creating a trauma-informed nation.

Reading the blogs from 'see me, hear me' on the Epione page, I was really inspired. Lee suggested this could be a way for me to do what I've always wanted to do – use my story to help others. Usually I would have said 'no way', but something felt right inside. I believed this was something I could do. It was also very serendipitous, as I had attended an event in 2019 held by Epione and had been left so inspired that I thought this could be the sign I was looking for to add another layer to my healing journey. At that event, I had also met my hero, Madeleine Black. Something felt so right about doing this.

I had to condense my story into 1000 words. I found this very difficult as there was so much I wanted to include, but what I wanted more was to share my message of hope and that healing can be possible, even though for many years I had not believed this to be true. I wanted to give someone else hope the way that Karen, Lee and Madeleine had given hope to me.

My blog was published on the 6th of March 2021, International Women's Day. I received lots of support from Alex O'Donnell, the co-founder of Epione. I had submitted my blog in February, yet he had waited until International Women's Day to share it. It felt very weird sharing this with a man. I had avoided the opposite sex like the plague since my attack, yet here I was sharing my deepest, darkest thoughts with a man and trusting him that it would work out ok. Alex has provided support ever since I agreed to share my blog and has welcomed me into his trauma thriving community, which I am very grateful for.

So this is what I have written so far on my blog, which can be found on the Epione website:

> *When I started writing the blog, I wasn't prepared for the feelings that would come back. My initial writing left me feeling triggered and panicked that I wasn't as far along in my healing journey as I'd thought.*

*I have read so many stories about how people have healed from trauma and wished so badly that I could be like them. I would always skip to the part that said how they did it, how did they heal from trauma? I so desperately wanted someone to tell me how to do that, because I hadn't found the answer. The reality is there is no real answer, no quick fix, everybody's journey is different and in actual fact healing is messy and very painful.*

*At age 21, I felt on top of the world, I don't think I ever remembered being happier, everything in my life was going 'just right'. What was to unfold next would lead me to a world I could never have imagined, full of pain, fear, trauma, shame, guilt, disgust and self-loathing and so much more.*

*It was Burns night 2003 and I was out celebrating my friend's 21st. I started to feel unwell and decided to go home. One of the girls I was with said that she would come with me, but I insisted that she didn't. I have spent many years blaming myself for this simple decision....why did I leave alone, why didn't I just let my friend come with me? If I had let her come, this horrific event would never have happened. It has taken me long time to process that I was not the one to blame for this!*

*When I left, I very quickly got a sense of someone behind me. Before I got a chance to look round or process that feeling, I was grabbed from behind and dragged down a lane. I thought my brain was going to explode with fear. I had no idea what had happened or what was about to happen.*

*That night, I was gang-raped by two men and left for dead. I had been subjected to four counts of rape in every part of my body that they could violate. I was stabbed, I was unconscious at times and literally felt broken inside and out. There are no words to describe the level of fear I felt that night – I thought I was going to die. It's amazing where your mind goes to whilst you are being raped and facing death. I was worried about who would find me, how would my family cope. At other points I seemed to come out of my body and view my attack as if I was sitting on top of the roof above me. Latterly, my fear that I was going to die became a desperate wish that it would just happen, then it would be over.*

*The rapists not only abused my body in ways that no women should be subjected too, they also abused my mind. Things that were said to me, the mind games they played with me and the threats that were put upon me saw me spiral into nearly two decades of horrendous guilt and shame, self-loathing and self-destruction. This has been a major part of my journey, learning about perpetrators and nothing I could have done that night could have stopped what happened.*

*It wasn't what I was wearing, what I did, if I had been drinking, if I had left alone. None of that was the cause of my rape – the rapists were the cause. I was silenced and unable to find my voice because of their actions and threats, which made me too scared to tell anyone. I was living in a silent hell that no one knew about.*

*I had dipped in and out of counselling, but had never truly addressed what happened to me. In 2017, an event at work triggered me back into my world of trauma. I had never connected with my trauma or worked through it to process what happened to me and the true impact that it had on me as a person. I went back to therapy in 2018 and this was where the hard work began. I could not find words to talk about what had happened, they were stuck in my throat and not allowed to come out. I felt very frustrated with myself and at times like I was losing my mind.*

*I also learned something else about my trauma – that your body remembers what your mind does not. I started to experience what is known as somatic pain. When I started to talk about certain points in my story, my body seemed to remember the pain it had experienced that night (which I had shut out!) and I began to relive it. It's hard to imagine how your brain can shut off from pain, but when pain and trauma become too much, it switches off to protect and help you survive. I do believe that if my mind had not disassociated that night, then I would not be here today.*

*In the last few years, I have been introduced to mindfulness by an amazing lady who has made a huge impact on my life. I've never been able to focus on the 'present moment', I was constantly living on high alert, worried about what was going to happen or reliving what had happened. 'Grounding' has helped me to come back into the present moment when my mind gets engulfed by my trauma. This sounds easy, but I have practised it for 2 years and still need help to do it at times. I have also learned to practise gratitude and come from a place of love and not hate. This has really helped me work on changing my mind set and my thought processes.*

*The men who raped me were continuing to live on in my head, but I now know that I have the power to change that narrative. This is where I found my fight to work towards living my best life in spite of them. My hope is that I can learn to live alongside my trauma and use it for a purpose, to help and support other women who have experienced similar trauma. I can still be triggered by what happened to me – and I'm learning that that's ok, it's how I respond and get myself back on track that is important. I've also learned that this will never go away, it has been such a major part of my life up until now, but it does not mean that I need to be defined by it. I am working on getting to a place where my hope is greater than my fears. Some days I can smash it and 'feel the fear and do it anyway' and other days I can be consumed by the fear. These are the days when I know that by pushing myself through it, I am helping to rewire the part of my brain that has been taken over my trauma.*

*In 2020, I had decided that I was not entering another decade with this consuming my life. I achieved lots in 2019, but I also saw myself in some very dark places. I was right in the middle of processing my story when the world seemed to be heading towards its own trauma – Covid 19. My anxiety levels reached stratospheric levels over the fear of how I would cope without my support network, without my weekly meetings with my mindfulness coach, having to be stuck at home with nowhere to go. This may have been the greatest lesson/opportunity I have ever been given, because just as the country went into lockdown, I contracted the virus. I quickly deteriorated and became very unwell. I found it difficult to breath, which triggered painful memories of not being able to get a breath that night. I also believed I was going to die – another painful memory I had not processed.*

*Fast forward and I feel like I've spent a year fighting for recovery – again! I was diagnosed with long Covid and have been plagued with ongoing symptoms. What this year has done for me though is, it has made me stop. Literally stop! This is the first time I've stopped to look my trauma straight in the eye. During this time, I have been given the opportunity to reconnect with my 21-year-old self, the girl I had blamed for what had happened. I now know that this girl was nothing but an innocent victim.*

*One of the worst parts of my attack was that two men stripped me of my identity and I have had to spend the last 18 years fighting to get it back. I have now learned that the core parts of me could never be taken away by them and these are the parts that have got me here today. I have fight, I have strength, I have resilience, I have determination and I may not always feel it, but I have a bravery inside me that has kept me going this entire journey.*

*Moving into 2021, I am determined to reclaim my body back and overcome the somatic pain and the panic around it. As for moving on with my life – I'll leave that up to the universe.*

The response I got from my blog was completely overwhelming. I had finally let go of that secret to the world. I had messages from people on social media I knew who were heartbroken to read what I had written and had had no clue about it. I also connected with people who had been in similar positions and found myself being the one to offer advice to others. Who was this person? In no way was I healed, or able to tell people how wonderful life was after trauma. However I was real and honest, and I think that's what made people connect to my story.

A few people didn't know what to say to me, and that was ok. I'm not sure I would have known what to say to someone in my position. But I no longer felt ashamed that this was my story. I was overwhelmed with comments on my strength, bravery and determination and for once I didn't instantly shut them down. I sat with those compliments and could really feel myself thinking, wow, you have been through a lot of shit!

When I look back at the last paragraph in my blog, I could not be more blown away: *Moving into 2021, I'll leave that up to the universe!* Well, look what has happened this year. I could never have planned for it, a lot of it I would never have wanted, but it has all got me to a place I had been searching for so long. I realised that letting go was possible!

CHAPTER 24

# Reclaiming my body

*'...and I said to my body softly. 'I want to be your friend'. It took a long deep breath and replied 'I have been waiting my whole life for this.' – Nayyirah Waheed*

I had started work way back with Karen on the somatic pain I was experiencing. It's something I know much more about now, but I still struggle with not having all the answers of how to fix it.

My body and mind became two separate things to me. This was where the disconnect from myself happened. The gap became wider and wider, until I was completely lost and didn't know who I was any more. I didn't want to know my body. My body reminded me of what happened and I was in absolute denial, wanting it to go away, wishing it could be different.

When trauma occurs in the body, the brain is flooded by stress hormones and your brain decides which route it is going to take to survive. Even if your body has decided to shut off that part of the brain that remembers, your body also remembers. Your body remembers on a cellular level and in my case, my body began remembering before my mind did. This was my body's way of telling me what my mind was refusing to recognise.

When your body remembers at a different time from your brain, it can make you feel like you are going crazy. I did not have the knowledge I have now about what trauma does to your brain. I genuinely thought I was going insane and was going to end up hospitalised. I could not understand why I would suffer these extreme pains in places I couldn't understand. I was referred to gynaecology to rule out anything sinister and going for appointments was a trauma in itself, but every test I had came back negative. This was when I started to realise this was my body's way of getting my attention. I was going to have to allow my body and mind to collide in order to heal. They had both lived through the same experience, so it was time to bring them together again.

At the end of 2019, Lee suggested a treatment that her friend Sally did called Bowen Therapy. I'm not really sure how to describe this, but it is an alternative healing therapy and soft tissue treatment that uses different moves to realign the body.

For nearly 15 years, I had been having ongoing problems with reccurring urine infections – or what I perceived to be urine infections. I had tests carried out by my GP and even had a procedure carried out in hospital to stretch my urethra in a bid to try and alleviate my symptoms. Most of the time, the urine tests would come back clear, so nobody could really find an explanation for this. My work with Karen made me start looking more at the impact of trauma on the body and this could have been one of things that had been affected by trauma. I became more aware of how much I tensed the muscles in this area, even when I hadn't realised I was doing it.

One of the main reasons for trying this alternative therapy was to try and address the somatic pain I was experiencing in the areas of the body where I had been so badly injured. Nothing else seemed to be working, and I was desperate to try anything. As I had found out with my work with Karen and Lee, my body's way of coping with extreme stress was to pass out, shutting down from what was happening. My body had not caught up with the fact that it was no longer in danger and didn't need to use this response any more.

I was very anxious on my first appointment, so Lee explained everything about my trauma and the somatic pains I had been having and where was a 'no go' area to touch. Sally was so understanding and said that I was totally in control of the treatment. My body was so tense during this first treatment that I don't know how Sally would have been able to get her magic through to my muscles. I remember feeling really emotional and shaky during it and afterwards felt like it hadn't really worked. The next few days I felt worse, but Sally told me this was a typical response as it was the body's way of working with the treatment.

The more sessions I had with Sally, the more I trusted her to try moves on different parts of my body. There was a particular move that I witnessed Sally do on Lee called the pelvic drainage, which involved a series of moves on the pelvic bone. This was as close as I was ever going to get to having someone help me in this area where the damage felt trapped. If anything was going to help these cells heal, I hoped this would be it. After several months, I found the courage to give it a go.

Of course my body reacted in the only way it knew how – I passed out on the bed. I would feel transported back to that night, totally unaware of where I was or who was around me. I would come back round again feeling panicked and disoriented. I was mortified. I was used to Lee seeing me like this and that was bad enough, but I couldn't believe I had just done this in front of someone I hardly knew. Yet Sally's response was one of total understanding and compassion for what I had been through.

Lee knew how to make my body feel safe again and brought me back to the present moment. It then became a mission for me to try and get as far as I could with the treatment without fainting. I could see some small windows of change with regard to the pain for the few days after the treatment. Whilst it hadn't gone away, I felt hope that something was changing.

It was during one of my sessions that I remembered some of the trauma that I had obviously buried very deep. It was something that I had no memory of whatsoever, but made so much sense once I pieced it all together.

I had had a clicky pelvis since the day I started with Sally and it never really bothered me. It was not a sore pain, it was just uncomfortable. During one session we laughed about it as she seemed to knock my leg out of position and couldn't get it back in. However as this move progressed, something in my head felt uncomfortable with it, but I wasn't sure what it was.

During one treatment, I had a flashback that would explain so much to me in terms of details within my story. As Sally pushed my left leg back towards my stomach, I felt a sharp pain going up my back passage and a feeling of not being able to breath. I was not able to share any of this with Sally or Lee – partly because I couldn't put words to it and partly because I did not want to acknowledge the reality of it. What unfolded from that flashback is that I had been raped anally in this position that I had not been aware of (or ready to come to terms with) and this clicking in my pelvis was probably the result of such a forceful impac.

For many years I had experienced a pounding pain on the right side of my head. I assumed it was migraine, although there was no rhyme or reason to when it would come. Normally the migraines I suffered from were hormonal, but this felt different. Again, during sessions with Sally, it came back to me that I had been kicked repeatedly in my head – the right side. I had no memory of this happening, but my head clearly remembered. Sally has been able to perform some moves on this area and these pains have practically gone.

I have continued to work with Sally since 2019 (minus periods of lockdown) and I am now so much more comfortable with her working on my body. I do still struggle with certain moves, but the benefit of the treatment certainly outweighs this struggle. I have now got to a place where I can fight against my brain's urge to shut down and faint and am able to bring myself back with Sally and Lee's support. I still suffer from somatic pain on some level and am still not sure on what the answer to this is for me, but I continue to work with Sally in the hope that one day, my mind and body will be truly reconnected 100 percent of the time in the present moment. It has been during the work with Sally that I have been able to piece together more of my story and helped me bring my mind and body together to help me heal.

CHAPTER 25

# The turning point – finding myself

*'And one day she discovered that she was fierce and strong and full of fire and that not even she could hold herself back because her passion burned brighter than her fears.'* – Mark Anthony

August 2021 saw me catapulted to a new level of darkness. I had been really struggling over the last few months with flashbacks and reliving memories that I thought I had processed. The start of the year had been going so well for me, but like most trauma survivors, I had trained my brain to be aware that good feelings don't last and the bad times will return. This was exactly what happened.

Unfortunately, Lee had been unwell and had to make the difficult decision to end her coaching work and our working relationship. I knew how difficult this must have been, and I totally respected her decision. I had grown to love her more as a friend now and only wanted what was best for her. However this left me with an overwhelming sense of fear and panic. This was another person who was leaving and not able to see my journey through to the end. I could see no way out. I felt I was too complicated to help. I made people who tried to work with me ill.

The narrative in my head was that there was no person out there who would ever be able to see me through this, because I was not meant to get to the end. The journey was too difficult, and this was the sign to say that this was as far as I could go. My rational brain allowed me to see that Lee was unwell and was doing exactly as she should be doing – taking care of herself to get her well again. However, cortisol, adrenaline, stress, anxiety, everything had just flooded my brain and body again and this time I didn't have Lee to pull me back.

My world descended into chaos again. I felt like the rug had been pulled from under me and began to feel panic that I don't ever remember experiencing before. This decision was the one I had been dreading most since I started working with Lee – that a therapeutic relationship would be cut short AGAIN, for the fifth time. I had never known what it was like to get to the point of working with a therapist/coach where I chose to end it, as this had always been someone else's decision. I did not know how I would be able to go on without Lee's support as she had been my rock for nearly three years. In reality I would probably never have chosen to leave any of my relationships with my therapists. They had all become such a safety blanket for me that in hindsight, I would probably always have needed a push of some sort for me to move on.

I was plagued by a rollercoaster of emotions, fear, panic, loss and grief, and then felt an overwhelming sense of guilt that I could be so selfish as to be thinking of this when someone I had grown so close too and classed as a friend was suffering too . The thought of losing Lee as a friend was more unbearable than losing her as a coach, and I did not know what was going to happen with our relationship.

The next few weeks saw me descend deeper and deeper into despair, feeling I was not going to make it. I had totally lost control. I was not able to hide this from anyone, like I usually did. I broke down to Trudy and to my mum one night (which I had never done) and told her how scared I was that I could not get through this without Lee. Trudy, who had been by my side, reassured me that she never has and never would go anywhere. I believed her and knew that she would be there for whatever I needed, but the problem was that I did not know what that was.

I reached out to a few other people, but they all had their own reasons as to why they could not help me at that time. It seemed like there was door after door being shut in my face. I remember thinking – you see adverts on TV and social media about people who have taken their own life, and no one around them knew how bad they had felt, always encouraging people to reach out. Here was me trying to tell people how bad I felt and no one was listening or able to help me.

Before I knew it, my body and mind had given up. I couldn't cope with the feelings any longer and without a care for what I might be leaving behind, I started to take some tablets in a bid to end my life. I felt a sense of relief that this feeling would soon be over. That echo of doom, that feeling of despair had now gone. I knew that I could not go on any further and would soon be at peace, mentally and physically. I could feel myself starting to drift into a state of unconsciousness.

Looking back, I am plagued with guilt that I could have come so close to putting Lucy and my family and friends through this, but no one could have understood the torment in my mind. The physical imprint of trauma had healed long ago, but as most survivors know, the mental torment that you are left with is often much worse than the attack itself.

I don't know what happened, but something inside me hit panic mode again about leaving Lucy and I immediately got up to make myself sick. My memories are very vague from this point. I remember speaking on the phone to someone from the Samaritans. I also reached out to Rape Crisis, but could not bring myself to speak to anyone. The next few hours and days are a blur at this point. I was in my bed ill (with a 'sickness bug'), consumed with guilt, fear and terror. I could not tell anyone about this and still did not know how I was going to get on, but I knew that for Lucy, I had to do something.

Lee had planned to do an ice bath breathing workshop at the Vortex Centre for wellbeing. I asked if I would be able to join her and her friend. I felt very weird being around Lee, as I still did not know where we stood in our relationship and I was scared I was going to make her feel worse by seeing me. However, we decided to go together – I was desperate to try anything that could make me feel better. I can honestly say, this workshop changed my life.

It is very difficult to describe what happened in this workshop – you really had to be there to understand the full impact. James McFadden, the man who was running the course, initially spoke to us about his reason for doing this and how breath work had literally saved his life. He too had faced significant trauma and life-altering mental health issues. James carried out a meditation for me, followed by several breathing exercises. I have done lots of mediations over the years, but this one blew my brain. James took our bodies on a journey of pure relaxation and asked us to reflect on when we felt loved and to really find the core of who we were.

The tears were streaming down my face into my ears as I truly got to a place where I thought (and felt) genuine love for myself. This had never happened before! I could feel something inside changing, possibly an acceptance of what had happened. I told myself that none of this was my fault and that I was a good person. I cried for what I had been through and for the first time ever, I felt sorry for my pain, my suffering, my journey. I thought of the two men who had done this to my body and mind and felt an overwhelming sense of – no more! You will no longer have the power in my mind to control me! What you did to me will not define who I am today or who I will become in the future!

I also really felt a sense of peace about the transition that was happening in the relationship between Lee and me. I knew that if we were meant to continue as friends, then it would happen and if we weren't, then I would be eternally grateful for what she had done for me. It also allowed me to see that it didn't matter how many counsellors I looked to for help, the real help I needed was from within. I needed to start relying on myself and know that I could help myself out of dark places. I could talk myself out of panic attacks, I could reassure myself when my inner critic took over. This was the 'me' that I had been on this journey to find and unfortunately, nobody could do this part for me. It was time to go it alone.

The breathing exercises that went along with this workshop have had an immeasurable impact on my ability to self-soothe and reduce panic. Simply focusing on the breath, focusing on the here and now was what was going to keep me here. These were all techniques that both Karen and Lee had taught me, but only now did I feel that it had all fallen into place.

I remembered years ago that my friend and yoga teacher had told me about a 'tool-belt' she had that helped her through times of struggle. It involved many strategies that would help her find strength to get through whatever came along. I visualised this tool belt and reflected on what I would have in mine to help me get through this next part. I had loved yoga at one time and found a real sense of calm from doing it. Having Covid has limited the exercise I am able to do because of its impact on my lungs, but I am hoping that I can get back to it. I also have mindfulness strategies that I have learned along the way – practising being in the present moment, getting out into nature, practising gratitude, doing meditation, noticing unhelpful thoughts and what to do with them. I have a wealth of knowledge in my head, I now just need to have the confidence in myself to continue the work and use what I need when I need it.

I had also started cold water dipping that year as a way of managing my thoughts and my body. The science behind this is that by entering the cold water, you put your body into a different kind of stress and change the chemistry within your brain. For me, the cold water has helped my mind focus on what my body can do. It helps me clear my thoughts. When I come out I feel a sense of accomplishment that I have been able to override the thoughts that tell me to run for the hills, and use my brain and my breathing to keep focused. It also makes my body feel totally rejuvenated and energised – not feelings that I usually have indoors.

I have a handful of special friends in my tool belt that I will continue to feel grateful for and I know they will continue to be there for me as I move on to this next chapter. My tool belt is actually very well resourced. I have gained so much knowledge and strategies from the people I have worked with along the way that I now need to continue using them and making them proud.

Looking back reflectively, the decision that initially came from Lee was probably the push from the universe that I had needed to go in the direction I had been avoiding during my healing journey. This next stage took me to a place deeper inside where I had to learn to rely on ME, no one else. I had to find that place where I was able to see my own worth and continue to heal from my trauma without relying on other people to do it for me.

It was never going to be anyone else who got me to the 'end

of this journey'; it was always going to be my responsibility and my fight and determination that would get me to this point. It also made me look deep inside to find the person I really was, and I was finally able to reunite the two people inside my head with love, kindness and acceptance.

I feel that I have now accepted that the past cannot be fixed or changed, and I realise that I had been searching for this in every counsellor I had worked with. I was hoping that someone in a professional role would be able to fix what had happened so that I would not be able to feel and remember any more. What happened happened, and I will never be able to change that, but what I can change is how I move on from it.

I remember begging Lee and Karen to tell me how to let go as I physically and mentally did not know how to do it. Lee would tell me that it would just happen. I wouldn't be able to plan it, I wouldn't be able to force it, it would just happen one day and that I would know. Again, she was right – it just happened.

CHAPTER 26

# Life begins at 40

*'You've always had the power my dear, you just had to learn it for yourself.'* – The Wizard of Oz

I had been dreading turning 40 all year. Not for any reason in particular, I just didn't want any fuss. I had struggled the last few months and felt tired of it all. I'd felt mentally and emotionally drained and was only just finding my strength and drive again. I didn't want anything to trigger a setback.

However, the people around me refused to let this go without a celebration of me and my special birthday. One of my birthday celebrations actually included a day out in Glasgow. I knew deep inside that this day was either going to be a game changer or a disaster. Lee, knowing my love of Disney and New York, had a planned a day that encompassed them both. We went to a Disney 'boozy brunch' not that far from where my attack took place. I felt that this was a final gift from Lee the coach to show me how far I had come and that I could face whatever was thrown at me.

The boozy brunch was amazing. It was Disney galore – music, singing, dancing. I just loved it and got totally lost in the moment of having fun with a special group of ladies. The ladies had spoiled me with gifts, balloons and a tiara and made me feel like a real-life Disney princess. I loved it!

The next part of the day was moving on to a New York-themed cocktail bar. This involved walking to a different destination which wasn't too far, but again, it took me out my comfort zone and had the potential to trigger me and ruin what had been achieved so far. Thankfully, all three ladies who were with me knew what I was facing and simply held my hand and got me to where we were going. I had done it. I had enjoyed a whole day and evening in Glasgow, completely letting go and enjoying myself. Another challenge that I completely smashed, and I was buzzing.

I actually had the most amazing birthday I could have asked for. I was spoiled with love and kindness from everyone around me that I loved. I got lots of new equipment for my new hobby of paddle boarding and cold-water swimming (which was my new form of therapy!) I was gifted a weekend away with my favourite people and enjoyed simply being in that moment. I felt very blessed and very grateful.

Just before my 40th birthday, I felt I had let something go and I had a sense of peace and quiet determination to move forward. Since the workshop I had attended with James McFadden. I had found myself building on my strength and resilience. I was able to catch my thoughts and catch panic before it got to a stage where it overwhelmed me. It felt very powerful that I was able to do this on my own.

I have since sought 1:1 support from James and attended several of his workshops. I really warmed to his kind and caring personality and drive to help people find solutions to their mental health troubles through breath work, meditation and finding solace within. I find it quite ironic that the person who has finally got me to look within and beyond the trauma has been a man! I limit my involvement with men where I can, so the fact that I was drawn to James says a lot about who he is as person and how far I have come on my journey. James has really helped me reach a different level of peace and finding my worth within.

Moving on in my 40$^{th}$ year, I find myself feeling pangs of excitement for what may come next.

CHAPTER 27

# How I would help someone else

*"People don't need to be saved or rescued. People need knowledge of their own power and how to access it."– Unknown*

Healing from trauma can mean so many different things for different people. Each person's trauma is unique to them. There is no right or wrong way to get through/over any traumatic experience. There is no guide book that gives you step-by-step instructions for how to do it – believe me, I've looked!

That night, my logical brain shut down and my survival brain took over. In that split second, my brain had to make the choice of fight, flight, freeze or fawn. I didn't get to make that choice, my brain did, and luckily for me, it made the right one. Understanding this, owning it and accepting it have all been part of my healing process, but it was not easy.

Each person has to find their own path and their own strategies and do what is right for them. I lost my self, my power and part of my soul that night. I had to find a way to get them back, and it is really important that each survivor has the support to regain some control again, making their own decision and find their own way through the process of healing. This is a very isolating journey and there is no way around it, but the support that can be given by friends, family or service providers are crucial in helping that survivor find their way.

If I were to use my own experience and suggest what I have needed in my healing journey, it would be the following: time, love and kindness, being held physically and mentally, listening and hearing, no judgment and lots of compassion.

With the knowledge I now have about trauma, I don't believe I would have survived the recovery of the traumatic events of that night had I tried to process them back then. I disassociated for a reason and I truly believe that was to save my life. My brain could not have coped with any of what I have processed and learned to deal with in these last few years. I physically and mentally had to be in a safe place to be ready to do the work. And it has definitely been work! I can finally see how much courage I needed to take that step to enter into a world of healing that was uncertain and not guaranteed. For me the world of fear and misery became my norm, so stepping out of that 'comfort zone' was a huge risk, but such a worthy one.

If I could share some advice based on my experience to anyone who has experienced trauma or anyone working with someone who has experienced trauma, it is that time and patience are key. Time is needed to process what has happened, and this may be immediate or it could take weeks, months or years. Everybody's responses to trauma are so unique to their own circumstances that you cannot be expected to follow a set pattern. There also needs to be time to heal. This may be achieved with or without professional support, but be prepared for this not to be a quick experience. It is so important to have time to be in control and to take ownership of recovery. Making decisions can be very difficult and you may need to be supported initially, but this is how you rebuild the trust with yourself and take the power back.

For me, I also needed lots of time to accept love and kindness in my healing journey. I would say that only in the last few years have I been able to accept this and actually take comfort in it. I used to reject any form of physical touch. I found it very hard when people were kind to me, as my trauma had left me believing I did not deserve it. I could not understand why someone would want to hug a body that was contaminated, dirty and broken. However in the last few years, the connections I have made have shown me that being held physically and mentally have allowed me to feel heard, to feel safe and have offered calmness to my body. The love and kindness I have received from so many people on my journey has truly allowed me to connect with myself and with others on a different level.

Over the years I had built many walls around my heart, walls that made it very difficult for me to allow people in to support me. With the right connections and relationships, I was able to take the wall down, brick by brick. Trust is something that I have struggled with and I know it's a common feature of those struggling with trauma. Having someone that you can trust in, someone who understands your complicated emotions and can help you with triggers and reactions is the really practical support that can aid the healing process. Again this is where I had to give time, patience and understanding to myself and those around me. Doctors can prescribe medication to support with the chemical imbalance in the brain, but they cannot prescribe the connections that truly help you work through your trauma.

People talk about how hard it is to trust people after you've been hurt, but what people don't say is how hard it is for you to trust yourself. This has been one of the final pieces of the puzzle for me and is wrapped up in feelings of shame and low self-worth. It was only when I was finally ready to look at these aspects and reconnect with myself that I have been able to start trusting myself again. This is where my power lay.

I would also suggest that you need to be really aware of other people's opinions, be they those of family members, friends, doctors or service providers. Sometimes what other people think is right can overtake what the survivor may actually need. Back when it happened, I don't think I could have told anyone what I needed, but I do know that it wasn't listening to people's opinions about what they thought I should do, i.e. go to the police, seek medical advice, go for counselling, tell my family. All of these major decisions need to be made by the survivor. They may feel that they have totally lost control of their life, so any decisions they are able to make should be fully supported. This can very quickly give a sense of being listened to and taking some sort of control. It can be very difficult to watch if you are trying to support somebody and you feel you may know what's best for them. Guidance can be offered, but then there has to be acceptance of the decisions made by the survivor. We know our stories long before we will probably share, so for us, taking control of our decisions helps to retain that little bit of ourselves that we have left. Whilst the few people I told about my attack may have thought they were suggesting what was best for me, I was not ready, and that was the most important point. It took me a long time to be ready for any of this.

For someone who has experienced or is healing from trauma, being listened to is crucial. It's not just being listened to, but being heard. I have worked with various counsellors and visited many doctors and felt so unheard by certain ones. I was trying my best to tell a story and whilst I appreciate they are not mind readers, they were not picking up on the clues I was giving in my presentation, my behaviours and my silence. This may have been due to the fact that I was struggling to find words for what happened. I didn't want to accept what had happened and was not really in a place to share, but when I finally did make these connections, I genuinely felt heard – even when there were no words. That changes something inside you.

Not being judged is also vitally important for victims of trauma. There will be no greater judgement than the judgment you place on yourself. No one will make you feel worse than the way you make yourself feel, and if you have someone around you who adds to that feeling, they will never play a positive role in you healing.

I am lucky that no counsellor I've worked with has judged

me. The things I've shared would terrify anyone close to me, but not the people I have worked with. The four women I mentioned at the start have worked with me to try and ease the shame that I kept so firmly locked inside. Having a relationship where you can share your humiliation has been key to allowing me to work through the layers of guilt and shame that kept me you trapped in the past.

Finally, the most important lesson I have learned from this journey is that to heal from trauma, you really need to learn to love *you* again. You need to be kind to yourself when others haven't been, you need to not judge yourself, you need to listen to yourself, you need to get the right support and you need to practise self-care. The past cannot be changed, but the memories can fade with the training of the mind and this is something I have learned is so important in continuing with my healing.

My journey has taken me the long way round to find what people had been telling me all along, but I was never ready to listen to them. I needed to go through all the different stages in my journey to finally have the strength and insight that would ultimately lead me back to myself.

## CHAPTER 28

# I'll have the final say! My letter to the men who raped me

*'Strong women aren't simply born. We are forged through the challenges of life. With each challenge we grow mentally and emotionally. We move forward with our heads held high and a strength that cannot be denied, women who have been through the storm and survived. We are warriors!*

I have debated over whether to include this in my book. I wasn't sure that I wanted to give those two men the time and space and acknowledgment, as they don't deserve to be spoken about in any way. However, I also wanted to let other survivors know how I felt about the men who raped me, as I haven't really discussed this in my journey. There is no right or wrong way about how you 'should' feel – it is unique to the individual.

For a long time I have struggled with how I felt towards them, because what I did feel was nothing. Surely I am meant to feel anger, rage or hatred towards them. Or should I forgive them? I had also heard stories about people healing in this way and wondered that perhaps if I could just do that, then maybe I would heal faster. In the end I decided that forgiveness of my attackers was not something I could do. What I have learned to do is forgive myself. Most people question why I would ever have to do this, but unless you have experienced trauma in this way, it can be difficult to understand. I also saw a quote from Oprah Winfrey: *'Forgiveness is letting go of the hope that the past can be changed'*. This was the kind of forgiveness I needed for myself to be able to move on.

Disassociation was the cause of my feelings of nothingness. I had spent so long pushing away and not acknowledging any of my feelings that I did not know what or how I felt. As feelings started to surface, I realised that the major emotion I carried was still fear. I had become so paralysed by fear that no other emotion could get through to allow me to process my feelings towards the two men who did this to me.

A lot of people have questioned why I am not angry at them for what they did. Anger has never really been an emotion that I've associated with in terms of my thoughts towards them. All of the counsellors I have worked with have expressed their own feelings of anger towards them for what they did to me, but I could never allow myself to feel it. A lot of this was tied up in my own feelings of self-worth and it was easier for me to be angry at myself than to direct it towards them. Thankfully this is not the case now. I do on occasions have feelings of anger, however this is not an anger that consumes me. I now understand why I feel this way, I allow myself to feel it and I let it pass.

I had been asked by several professionals if I had ever thought of writing a letter to the 2 men that raped me. I would very quickly shut this idea down and point blank refused to even consider it. Again this was a fear based response that had to be worked through, but I have finally got there I have decided that I have the right to a response and a final say.

December 2021

**To the 2 men who raped me.**

From the minute you put your hand over my mouth to drag me down that lane, you took away my voice and silenced me. You silenced me way back then and have done for nearly the last 20 years, even when your hand was no longer there. But not any more, you do not own that power over me. I have found my voice and I am no longer scared to share my story, your threats no longer fill me with fear.

I wish I could have left a mark on your body, but nothing could compare to the scars you have left on mine, physically and mentally. I would love to know why you chose me that night, but I know no answer you could give me would ever help me make sense of your abhorrent behaviour.

I did not realise until writing this letter the feelings of anger I actually have for you both, however it is not the kind of anger that ever has or ever will overwhelm me. You don't own that power over me. The anger I have is justifiable anger for a crime that you both committed against me and to let this anger eat me up would only be hurting me – you both have done that enough, I do not need to do that to myself.

You were inside my body without my permission. You took something from me that was never yours to take. You took my innocence, my first experience of being with a man and made it something distorted, vile and torturous. This may have been a bit of fun for you both but for me it was so much more. I did not deserve that, no one does!

You took away the way I viewed the world and my sense of safety within this and shook it to the core. You left me feeling disjointed, ripped from myself, my safety and my sanity. You made me experience fear on a level I could never describe, which has lasted so much longer than the few hours of that night. I did not deserve that.

My trust was smashed, my worth was gone and you left me in a world of pain that was immeasurable. You had my life in your hands, I looked death in the eye. You had a level of power that no one has the right to over any other human being. I did not deserve that.

You stole the blessing of being able to carry a child for the first time and made it something shameful and disgusting and then ultimately the torment of your actions stole that dream of becoming a mother. You left me with an imprint on my brain and took nearly 2 decades of my life as I have fought to recover. I feel a sense of injustice that you both will never know any of this have simply walked away. I did not deserve that!

Some people are able to practice feelings of forgiveness towards their abusers and I admire people that can do this, however, this is not my path. I cannot forgive what you both did to me, but I can chose to forget you. Some people have suggested that you may not have had the easiest of experiences which may have shaped the way you turned out – I do not care!

I am a very caring and empathetic person and have a lot of understanding of how people's experiences can shape their future, but I can honestly say, I don't care what either of you may have went through in the past, you had no right to do this me.

I often think what you both may be doing now, if that night has had any significance on your life? But I know the answer to this is probably not. Do you even remember that hour or so of torture that you subjected me to on that night, was I one of many people that you have done this too? I don't know if you have managed to go on with your life as normal, but I know I certainly have not.

You will never really know the true impact of what you both did to me that night

Part of me hopes that you both feel some sort of torment about your actions, just like the years of torment you left me with, but I don't hold out much hope that you do. I will never forgive what you did to me, but through time, I hope to forget you. I will always be disgusted by the acts you committed against my body and mind, my spirit and my soul, but your actions will not define the person I am today.

You no longer hold that power over me. The memories of trauma you left on my brain that night cannot be undone, but the imprint can be changed. I have evolved into a person that I may never have been had that night not happened, but that is no thanks to either of you. That credit belongs to me and that hard work I have put in to heal from those few moments of pleasure you may have had.

You do not belong in my thoughts, in my body and in my soul and today I leave you both here, in this letter. I will continue to take my power back, making the rest of my life the best of my life, not because of you but in spite of you and this will be my best revenge against you both.

*Debbie*

CHAPTER 29

# Moving on – the next chapter

*'What is your best discovery? asked the mole. 'That I'm enough as I am' said the boy.' – Charlie Mackesey, The Boy, the Mole, the Fox and the Horse*

I thought there would be. All this time I had visualised the place I would get to when I 'got over' my trauma and say I was in a place I didn't remember being before, but I am under no illusion that the work I have carried out to get here could simply end. Through sharing experiences and connecting with other survivors of trauma I have become more aware that there is no end to healing, there is no 'getting over it', there is no 'getting to the other side'. Because that 'other side' does not exist, it will always be part of me. What I have realised is that you can work your way through your trauma so that you are no longer consumed by it and it no longer has power over your life.

I have come to realise that I was never broken, even after years and years of feeling broken inside. That was in fact hurt. I was hurt, I didn't need to be fixed, I needed to be healed. The healing journey I have been on over the last 19 years (more so in the last four years) has been something I thought was impossible. I never believed anyone who told me I would be ok again, that I would be able to feel peace instead of anxiety, love instead of fear, present instead of trapped. All of these things I never believed to be possible, yet here I am today, writing the last chapter of a book that I hope will be able help someone else one day and give them hope and strength to carry on.

I am in awe of Madeleine Black and the work she does to continue to support survivors, using her story to bring about change, being an advocate of support for so much that needs to be changed in our world with regard to women and their right to live a life free from abuse. Like Irene, like Karen, like Lee, they all have a gift in this world to try and make things better for people, and I really hope I can join them and impact other people's lives the way they have mine. These ladies have been in a relay race when it came to the work they were able to help me out with, each passing the baton to another for the different stages I needed them for. Although I found all of these endings very painful, I do know that this has been for a reason and they will all continue to be in my corner one way or another.

For me, the biggest part of my journey has been about connection: connection with myself and connection with others. I lost connection with my inner core. I lost the life I thought I was going to have. I not only lost the person I was that night, but I lost the person I thought I was going to be. Yet the true strength of that inner core was always there, as that was the strength that got me through every obstacle and hurdle in my way. I just couldn't see it.

I also would never have found my way back to myself had it not been for the connection I had with a few special people who have stuck around to see me get to this place. I have often felt like a burden on people, ashamed of how I was managing and ashamed to ask for help, apologising for how I was responding and reacting and guilty for not doing better. I now remind myself that the irony of this is that no one asked my permission before I was attacked, so I don't need to ask for permission for how I show up in life. I now see reaching out as an act of strength, rather than a defeat or failure.

Moving forward, I question – how do I stay healed? I know that like all trauma survivors, I will carry my trauma with me forever, but I will continue to be responsible for how this unfolds in the future. If things come up that knock me off track, I will remember that my success rate for getting through these times has been 100% so far. I have gained so many strategies, techniques and skills along the way, and they will simply add to my resiliency tool belt and help me get back on track again.

I find it quite strange that one of my biggest strategies for calming my emotional state has been breath work. It was something that I struggled with so much that night, not being able to get a breath or breathe normally and feeling suffocated, yet it has now become my superpower and can bring me back from most situations.

My inspiration for moving forward is obviously my precious

little girl Lucy, and I will continue to be everything I can be for her to make sure she has the best life possible. My other huge inspiration is for helping other people. I know that I am a good person. I am caring and kind and can empathise with people on many levels. I would love to use what I have been through to help other people find their way too, and I would finally feel that all of this pain and suffering has not been in vain.

But finally, my biggest inspiration is for myself. I deserve to have a life that's full of love and happiness and I am determined to make the rest of my life the best of my life, no matter what comes my way. I finally feel at peace with what's gone, at peace with what's now and at peace with what's to come.

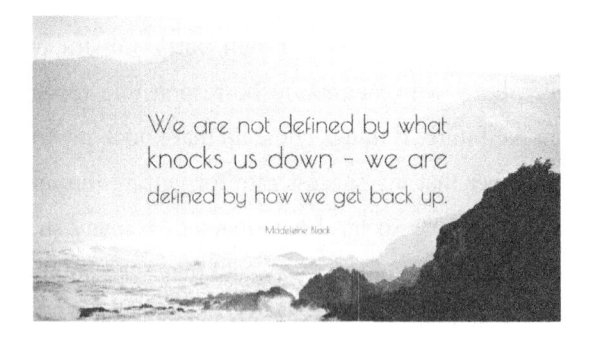

> We are not defined by what knocks us down – we are defined by how we get back up.
>
> Madeleine Black

The End

Printed in Great Britain
by Amazon